PASSION *for* JESUS

MIKE BRUMBACK

Passion for Jesus: Discovering Jesus Passion for You!
By Mike Brumback
Copyright 2018 • All rights reserved.

Exodus Christian Book Publishing
www.exoduschristianbookpublishing.com

No part of this book may be used or reproduced by any means, graphic, electronic, or mechanical, including photocopying, recording, taping or by any information storage retrieval system without the written permission of the publisher except in the case of brief quotations embodied in critical articles and review.

All Scripture quotations, unless otherwise noted are taken from the New King James Version®. Copyright © 1982 by Thomas Nelson, Inc. Used by permission. All rights reserved.

Scripture quotations marked (NASB) are taken from the NEW AMERICAN STANDARD BIBLE®, Copyright © 1960, 1962, 1963, 1968, 1971, 1972, 1973, 1975, 1977, 1995 by The Lockman Foundation. Used by permission.

Scripture quotations marked (NIV) are taken from the Holy Bible, New International Version®, NIV®. Copyright © 1973, 1978, 1984, 2011 by Biblica, Inc.™ Used by permission of Zondervan. All rights reserved worldwide. www.zondervan.com The "NIV" and "New International Version" are trademarks registered in the United States Patent and Trademark Office by Biblica, Inc.™

Scripture quotations marked (EXB) are taken from The Expanded Bible. Copyright ©2011 by Thomas Nelson. Used by permission. All rights reserved.

Cover Design by Exodus Design Studios
www.exodusdesign.com

ISBN: 9781726839716
Printed in the United States of America

CONTENTS

Introduction   i

1.	Discovering the Bridegroom God	1
2.	The Beauty of the Bride	21
3.	The Glory of Loving God	33
4.	The Seven Longings of the Bridal Paradigm	41
5.	The Embrace of Sonship	57
6.	The Throne of God	71
7.	The Beauty of God	87
8.	The Bridal Seal of Fire	97
9.	The Worthy Lamb of God	107

Other Products by Mike Brumback   **125**

INTRODUCTION

I want to personally thank Mike Bickle and the International House of Prayer of Kansas City for imparting the language and revelation of many things that are written in my book. In 1997, I went to a conference on Passion for Jesus in Kansas City. The worship that was led by David Ruis and Daniel Brymer was amazing. I remember Mike Bickle teaching on the Song of Solomon which I never heard before and the call to love Jesus with all your heart. It was powerful!

I had the honor of being a part of a small team that helped Mike Bickle birth and pioneer IHOPKC. It was from 1999-2011 that I soaked in the passion and desire of God's heart for me. I simply locked into the revelation of God's beauty, and my beauty in Him. Honestly, before moving to Kansas City, my paradigm of God was mostly distorted with negative thinking. I never thought He could be happy with me and believed He was always disappointed in me. But over the years, as I gazed and meditated upon a beautiful happy God who was on fire for me, He started to change my image and mindset of His personality. It was life-changing. But it didn't come overnight. There were many years of wrestling to embrace the truth, especially of my beauty in Him. I am still a work in progress.

If God could change my heart and mindset of who He is and who I am in His eyes, so He can do the same for you. If He could renew my image of an angry and cranky God to a happy God who smiles over me, so He can do the same for you. If He could take my cold heart and set my heart aflame with passion for Jesus, so He can do the same for you. He is no respecter of man.

Beloved, I am writing this book, so you can be awakened to a holy pursuit of Passion for Jesus. God can take your dull heart and revive you to have a lovesick heart for Him. You just need to believe, receive, and press in like never before. As you're faithful to do your part, He will definitely do His part. He will bring the transformation. You don't have to live with a cold heart before heaven. You don't have to live at a distance from your Beloved. There is hope for nearness and passion at a level you can't imagine.

Now just because I'm the author of my book "Passion for Jesus" does not mean I have it all together. I have actually been in the wilderness for some time. I haven't felt that closeness to God's heart that I had when I was at IHOPKC. I am not fasting and feeling the tenderness of the Holy Spirit that I am used to. My bridal love has had its ups and downs, more on the downsides, but I am still a lover of God! The fact that I'm writing this book shows me Jesus' strong passion for me, and He's using it to ignite holy passion in my spirit.

This is your story; it's your destiny. If there has ever been a time where we need passion for Jesus, it would be now. It is not later or some other time, but now is the set time. Life is short as time flies by so fast. I don't want to have any regrets when I stand upon the sea of glass like crystal. What about you? Do you feel the same way? I want the fullness and reward of what God has ordained for me. I want to be living and gazing upon the beauty of the Lord all the days of my life, just like King David.

It is my desire and prayer that this simple book on "Passion for Jesus" will set your heart on fire, and usher you into the beauty realm of God. You will be a prophetic voice calling the bride back to her first love. You will encourage and challenge God's people to be living for one purpose; it's called the glory of loving God in the first commandment. There is simply no other way to live. There is absolutely nothing on the earth that will satisfy your soul like Jesus, the Bridegroom God. He is madly and intimately in love with you. His gaze is upon you. He wants you to burn like He burns. You will never find what you're looking for until you discover what He is looking for. You will never enter your destiny until passion for Jesus becomes your destiny!

The premise of my book is built upon and found in 1 John 4. It's the key and secret to Passion for Jesus. Let this verse grab hold of you until you feel God's passion and fire over your life.

 *We love Him because He first loved us.*
1 John 4:19

If I were to ask you how to get passion for Jesus, what would be your answer? The answer I heard over the years was we need to read the Word of God, pray, fast, disciple the nations, fellowship, and be good stewards of what God has given us. Now this is a great list of the spiritual disciplines, but they should not be the primary way to get passion for Jesus. They need to be secondary. So, what should be the primary way to get passion for Jesus? **Passion for Jesus comes from discovering His passion for you!** That's the key to set your heart on fire for your Beloved.

It was John Wesley who was deeply moved by the passage in 1 John 4:19. He writes; "This is the sum of all religion. None can say more. Why should anyone say less?"

John the Apostle tells us that its Jesus who first loved us. He first pursued and reached out to us way before we reached out to Him. He planted the seed of divine love within us. His bloody crucifixion and supernatural resurrection shouts forth His passionate love for us. When we start focusing on Jesus' passion for us more than our passion for Him, our heart will be empowered and will come alive again. It's not enough to know in our mind of God's passionate desire for us, but we need to feel it deep within. It will cause us to live in voluntary obedience and not mandatory obedience. The spiritual disciplines won't be a burden anymore, but a profound delight. When we focus on God's commitment to us more than our commitment to Him, we will feel vibrant in our spirit.

Beloved, let's go for it together. Let's be the ones that devote ourselves to living and abiding in the flame of holy love and holy passion. Let's set our heart to remove all other passions within us and be conquered by Jesus passion for us. Let us be the ones who proclaim and impart the reckless love that burns in the heart of God to the nations. Passion for Jesus will be the banner over our lives!

CHAPTER 1
Discovering the Bridegroom God

You're probably familiar with hearing about Jesus as your Lord and Saviour, your King, Master, and Holy God. But have you ever heard or known Jesus as your Bridegroom? He is the Bridegroom God!

John the Baptist was the greatest man born on earth. That's how Jesus described him. But what is fascinating to know is how John found his greatest satisfaction and joy in his bridal relationship with Jesus; being a friend of the Bridegroom.

 *He who has the bride is the bridegroom; but the friend of the bridegroom, who stands and hears him, rejoices greatly because of the bridegroom's voice. Therefore this joy of mine is fulfilled.*

John 3:29

John was the first person to declare the beautiful Bridegroom God in the New Testament. He didn't see himself as a slave of God but as a friend. That was very personal to him. Do you see yourself as a friend of God? Do you have the confidence to come before His throne as a friend of the Bridegroom?

We know the Bible tells us in 1 John 4 that God is love, but do we know that God is a lover? That's the paradigm of knowing and encountering Jesus as a Bridegroom. Until we discover and start feeling on the inside "why" Jesus died on the cross for us, we will just be content to know that God is love. The Bible describes His love as a relentless burning fire. When it hits us that we were the ones that Jesus wanted even when we didn't want Him, and we were the ones He pursued even when we didn't pursue Him then our hearts will become empowered to love and serve Him with joy and vibrancy. Jesus is a lover who passionately sought after us while we never sought after Him, that's the power of the message of the Bridegroom God.

And they shall call them the Holy People, the Redeemed of the Lord; <u>And you shall be called Sought Out</u>, a City not Forsaken.

Isaiah 62:12

Characteristics of the Bridegroom God
1. **Beauty** - Song of Solomon 5:10-16
2. **Desire** - Song of Solomon 7:10
3. **Joy** - Isaiah 62:5
4. **Zeal** - Zechariah 8:2
5. **Passion** – Song of Solomon 8:6-7
6. **Tenderness** – Psalm 145:8
7. **Romance** – Hosea 2:19-20
8. **Jealousy** – Deuteronomy 4:24

Understanding the Message of the Bridegroom

The revelation and message of the Bridegroom God will cover the earth in the last days. He is not only a Bridegroom but a "ravished Bridegroom."

You have ravished my (Jesus) heart, My sister, my spouse; You have ravished my heart with one look of your eyes, with one link of your necklace.

Song of Solomon 4:9

The Hebrew word for "ravished" is *labab*. It literally means to be emotionally overcome with joy and delight and to be filled with strong emotion. The God of all power, wealth, and authority has emotions that are deeply moved as we set our gaze upon Him. Just "one look" focused on Him ravishes His heart. It doesn't take very much to move and impact God's heart like we think it does.

The ravished heart of God has a raging river of affections surging within His being. He is relentless in His pursuit of us. Not even the angels or seraphim before the throne have the capacity to ravish God's heart, but we do! Doesn't that amaze you? Do you understand who you really are in His eyes? Let me tell you who you are before the Bridegroom God. You are His rose, and you are awesome. Make sure you say it over and over. You're just speaking back what God says about you in the scriptures.

<u>I am the rose of Sharon</u>, *And the lily of the valleys.*

Song of Solomon 2:1

O my love, you are as <u>beautiful</u> as Tirzah, <u>Lovely</u> as Jerusalem, <u>Awesome</u> as an army with banners!

Song of Solomon 6:4

> *Who is she who looks forth as the morning, Fair as the moon, Clear as the sun, <u>Awesome</u> as an army with banners?*
> Song of Solomon 6:10

Do you notice the word "awesome" in both passages? I'm sure it's easy for you to say that God is awesome, but can you say that you are awesome? You're awesome because the awesome God lives and abides in you. When you believe you are awesome, you will start feeling confident and powerful in God's heart.

When we talk about Jesus as our Bridegroom God, we need to think of <u>5 aspects</u> of who He is and what His intentions are for us. Take some time and ponder over them to awaken your heart to passion for Jesus.

1. The Bridegroom God Desires a Bride to be with Him Forever

I love the word "desire." It unveils the heart and motivation of why Jesus came to the earth and passionately died on the cross for the human race. To be desired by God means to be wanted. Do you feel wanted by God or do you feel rejected by Him? Something makes us come alive again when we feel desired and cherished by the beautiful God who reigns upon His throne. It absolutely changes our life. It takes us from the pit of hopelessness and despair to the mountain of glory. We are the ones God likes. He really likes us. He really, really likes us. Before you continue reading, take a little time to speak out loud over, and over saying; "Jesus, here I am, your favorite one, the one that you like, it's me again."

Many believers define their lives by their struggle with sin and failure, and not by the burning desire of the One who loves them unconditionally. We are not the sum total of our most recent struggle. We are loved by God and our lovers of God. It's who we are, and it's what we do.

The God of desire is not tolerating you but desires you for who you are, and not what you can do for Him. You never have or never will be a burden to Jesus, the Bridegroom God. Not only does He desire you even in your personal struggles and issues, but will always desire you throughout eternity. He simply wants to be with you and reveal His deep secrets to you. He desires that you behold His glory. He has many things, many secrets He wants to share with you.

 *<u>Father, I desire</u> that they also whom You gave Me may be with Me where I am, <u>that they may behold My glory</u> which You have given Me; for You loved Me before the foundation of the world.*

John 17:24

The question we must ask ourselves is: does the God we worship and serve have deep feelings inside Him? If so, are those feelings positive or negative towards us in our relationship with Him? It seems like we so easily buy into the lies of the enemy about who we are in God's eyes. We wrestle to embrace the truth that He desires us and really likes us for who we are. The enemy continually tells us how dark and sinful we are, yet the Bridegroom God is shouting like a trumpet how special and unique we are as His bride. When we see Jesus as a Bridegroom God, it will enable us to see ourselves as His cherished bride.

Did you know that Jesus boasts and talks about our hidden beauty being formed in us before the Host of Angels? He has so many good things to say about us because that's the heart and desire of the Bridegroom God. The most important question we must ask the Lord is this: "what are you thinking, what are you feeling towards me, I have to know?" Give much time and thought to allow Him to answer you. I believe you will be so surprised and stunned at what He has to say to you. Because your His friend why wouldn't He answer you?

The Bridegroom of Desire

What would our Christian life be like without worshiping a God who has deep feelings and affections? Imagine coming before Him and expressing your love and devotion to Him and never feel His affections back. It would be absolutely miserable. It would be like the earth having no color in it. It would be like singing music without feeling the rhythm of it. It would be like pouring out your love to your spouse and never receiving love back. It would be one-sided.

Do you believe that God is for you and not against you? Do you believe His passion for you is much stronger than your passion for Him? There's no one more concerned about your personal life, career and ministry than Jesus, the Bridegroom. There is no one more intimately acquainted with everything going on in your life than Him (see Psalm 139:1-4). He wants you to be strongly convinced deep within.

If God could desire and accept us in our absolute darkness before we were saved, why wouldn't He desire and accept us now that we belong to Him? He desires us in the lowest pit, and He desires us in the highest glory of our lives. He is the Bridegroom of desire. Hallelujah!

 *I am my beloved's, And <u>His desire is toward me</u>.*

Song of Solomon 7:10

Hosea the prophet is a picture of the Bridegroom God in the book of Hosea. God told Hosea to go and marry a prostitute (Gomer), so He could feel the unending love for the nation of Israel. Gomer spent her entire life in harlotry. She never knew what true love was. She only knew that she had no value or significance in life and was used and abused at the hands of men. She could not have been at a lower place in her life. Just when probably everyone had given up on

Gomer, we see the God of burning desire, the One who has the capacity to be ravished who steps on to the scene. He was not embarrassed to stoop low in her dark pit and cloth her in white garments and give her a whole new life.

Nobody wanted Gomer, but God did. He saw something in her that no one else saw. He didn't see where she was as a prostitute but saw where she would be in the future as a bride. The Bridegroom God invited His friend Hosea to share with Him in His sufferings by asking him to take a "wife of harlotry" (see Hosea 1:2). Here is a question that always puzzles my mind. How could a Holy God ask a holy prophet to marry a filthy prostitute? Therein lies the mystery of the Bridegroom God.

Listen to what Isaiah the prophet boldly declared in his generation. It is more than words on paper, but its life-changing revelation from the burning desire of the Bridegroom God. The message proclaimed is the new special name that will be given to you - "Hephzibah." It means God's delight is in her.

 *You shall no longer be termed Forsaken, Nor shall your land any more be termed Desolate; But you shall be called <u>Hephzibah</u>, and your land Beulah; <u>For the LORD delights in you</u>, And your land shall be married. .For as a young man marries a virgin, So shall your sons marry you; And as the bridegroom rejoices over the bride, <u>So shall your God rejoice over you</u>.*

Isaiah 62:4-5

The Bridegroom God is pictured rejoicing over His people, the nation of Israel. He's not pictured rejoicing over what they had accomplished for Him; He's simply rejoicing over the ones that are married to Him for life. This prophetic word is not only for God's chosen people in Isaiah's day but is a direct word to you as His cherished bride. Don't ever forget your new name spoken by the Bridegroom "Hephzibah." I will get more into the revelation of God's delight and gladness later in this chapter.

2. The Bridegroom God has Invited Us to a Wedding

The second aspect of discovering Jesus as a Bridegroom is being convinced that we have been invited to a royal wedding. It was John the Apostle who had this revelation from the throne room of heaven.

 *Let us be glad and rejoice and give Him glory, for the marriage of the Lamb has come, and His wife has made herself ready." And to her it was granted to be arrayed in fine linen, clean and bright, for the fine linen is the righteous acts of the saints.*

Revelation 19:7-8

Look at the bride's response on her wedding day. She is pictured rejoicing and fully prepared to meet her Beloved face to face. It's a great day for her, and it's a really great day for the Bridegroom. He has been patiently anticipating this glorious day from the beginning of time.

The Bible has one grand theme running through the pages; a wedding! Jesus' public ministry began at a wedding, and His public return will end with a wedding. The marriage of the Lamb is the highest calling of God's heart. Everything we have ever gone through and endured for Him has led to this grand day. It will be a unique day as Jesus finished the good work in His bride, to reign in partnership with Him. The marriage of the Lamb is called the day of the gladness of Jesus' heart in the book of Song of Solomon.

 *Go forth, O daughters of Zion, And see King Solomon (Jesus) with the crown with which his mother (church) crowned him On the day of his wedding, The day of the gladness of his heart.*

Song of Solomon 3:11

Do you ever think about where you are headed in your future? Have you spent any time in your spiritual journey pondering at the big picture of your life, and where this whole thing about life is taking you? Beloved, you are going to a wedding! It's not just any ordinary wedding because it's not been prepared by man. This wedding is the future joy that was set before Jesus as He endured the cross (see Hebrews 12:2). It is the wedding of all ages, and you will be the center of attention before the heavenly hosts of angels. You will be clothed in white garments, presented faultless in His holy presence. You are no longer married to anyone but the Bridegroom, and He will never divorce you!

How does it make you feel that out of the whole world you have been personally invited and chosen by God Himself to a noble wedding with Him? History began with a bride and Bridegroom in the garden, and history will end with a bride and Bridegroom in the eternal city. That's your story because you're caught up in His story. Forever you will serve and reign with the Lamb of God, as you behold His glorious face.

 *And there shall be no more curse, but the throne of God and of the Lamb shall be in it, and His servants shall serve Him. <u>They shall see His face</u>, and His name shall be on their foreheads. There shall be no night there: They need no lamp nor light of the sun, for the Lord God gives them light. And they shall reign forever and ever.*

Revelation 22:3-5

3. The Bridegroom God Possesses Infinite Beauty

The third aspect of discovering Jesus as a Bridegroom is knowing He possesses infinite beauty. I absolutely love the revelation of the Beauty of God. For many years in my Christian walk, I never thought that God is beautiful. Has it ever crossed your mind that God is absolutely beautiful? The scriptures are packed with many passages that unveil His beauty.

The beauty of God was the secret to King David's life. It was his passion and longing to be caught up in marveling, as he gazed upon the beauty of the Lord. Beholding is all about encounter!

> *One thing I have desired of the LORD, That will I seek: That I may dwell in the house of the LORD All the days of my life, To behold the beauty of the LORD, And to inquire in His temple.*
>
> Psalm 27:4

John the Apostle gives a description of the beauty of the Bridegroom (Son of Man) in Revelation 1. He received it when he was ninety years old. You're never too old, or it's never too late to have Jesus reveal his surpassing beauty to you.

> *Then I turned to see the voice that spoke with me. And having turned I saw seven golden lampstands, and in the midst of the seven lampstands One like the Son of Man, clothed with a garment down to the feet and girded about the chest with a golden band. His head and hair were white like wool, as white as snow, and His eyes like a flame of fire; His feet were like fine brass, as if refined in a furnace, and His voice as the sound of many waters; He had in His right hand seven stars, out of His mouth went a sharp two-edged sword, and His countenance was like the sun shining in its strength.*

And when I saw Him, I fell at His feet as dead. But He laid His right hand on me, saying to me, "Do not be afraid; I am the First and the Last. I am He who lives, and was dead, and behold, I am alive forevermore. Amen. And I have the keys of Hades and of Death.

Revelation 1:12-18

The Shulamite who becomes the bride gives a poetic description of Jesus, the Bridegroom God to the Daughters of Jerusalem in Song of Solomon 5. What stands out in this portion of scripture for us to understand is the Bridegroom God is altogether lovely, and the bride encounters Jesus as her Beloved, and her friend. This is what we so desperately need in our daily lives.

My beloved is white (radiant) and ruddy (dazzling), Chief among ten thousand. His head is like the finest gold; His locks are wavy, And black as a raven. His eyes are like doves By the rivers of waters, Washed with milk, And fitly set. His cheeks are like a bed of spices, Banks of scented herbs. His lips are lilies, Dripping liquid myrrh. His hands are rods of gold Set with beryl. His body is carved ivory Inlaid with sapphires. His legs are pillars of marble Set on bases of fine gold. His countenance is like Lebanon, Excellent as the cedars. His mouth is most sweet, Yes, <u>He is altogether lovely</u>. <u>This is my Beloved, and this is my friend</u>, O daughters of Jerusalem.

Song of Solomon 5:10-16

The beauty of God is a huge and vast subject to search out. There are so many different aspects to discover, but at the foundation is the revelation of His heart and character. That's what makes Him beautiful. It was Nehemiah the prophet who received this powerful truth and revelation. I call it the five pillars of God's heart. In chapter seven of my book, I will further develop the theme of the beauty of God. This is just a glimpse of His shining glory and beauty. Here are the 5 pillars of God's heart. Maybe some of you will write an article or a book on these permanent and unmoveable pillars.

1. Forgiving
2. Gracious
3. Compassionate
4. Slow to Anger
5. Abounding in Loving Kindness

 *...But You are a God of forgiveness, Gracious and compassionate, Slow to anger and abounding in lovingkindness; And You did not forsake them.*

Nehemiah 9:17 (NASB)

4. The Bridegroom God Overflows with Gladness Over His Bride

The fourth aspect of discovering Jesus as a Bridegroom is understanding that He overflows with gladness over His bride. If learning about Jesus as a Bridegroom filled with passion for me was difficult to embrace, how much more did I struggle with believing that God is happy and smiling over me with gladness. I never imagined that the God of the universe could actually be happy with me. Maybe He is happy with Billy Graham who just went to be with the Lord, or maybe He is happy with the pope, but happy with me, no way. I could only see a list of struggles and sins in my life. But the truth is that God is happy with me because it's His nature to be happy, and He sees me clothed in the beauty of His Son and His righteousness. He sees the fight in me that longs to please Him by resisting darkness. He sees the progress to holy abandonment and a holy pursuit for Him.

Beloved, Jesus the Bridegroom God is happy with you and rejoices over you with gladness. He sings His love songs over you to deliver you. Freedom is enjoying a happy God who shouts over you with prophetic songs from heaven. Take some time and start pondering and meditating upon the truth that your God is smiling over you even in your weakness. Imagine and picture a big smile breaking out on Papa's face when He looks at you. What do you have to lose? Listen to what the scriptures record in Zephaniah 3.

 *The LORD your God in your midst, The Mighty One, will save; He will rejoice over you with gladness, He will quiet you with His love, <u>He will rejoice over you with singing</u>.*

Zephaniah 3:17

The paradigm most common today is that of a God who is mostly mad or mostly disappointed with us in our relationship with Him. If you only think that God is constantly disappointed with you, then you have a wrong image and paradigm of who He is. Instead of focusing upon what you have done or haven't done, start focusing on His passion and commitment towards you, more than your passion and commitment towards Him. This will get your focus off yourself and on His character and emotions. Give much attention to the five pillars of His heart. It will help realign your ability to receive.

God's gladness and happiness is not some temporary mood that comes and goes like it does with us, but it's an eternal attribute within His heart. Jesus possesses gladness more than any other person in human history. The Bridegroom God is the happiest person you will ever meet. He possesses the anointing of gladness.

 *But to the Son He says: "Your throne, O God, is forever and ever; A scepter of righteousness is the scepter of Your kingdom. You have loved righteousness and hated lawlessness; Therefore God, Your God, has anointed You With the oil of gladness more than Your companions.*

Hebrews 1:8-9

The gladness of God and His enjoyment towards us does not mean that He agrees with every area of our lives. We just read that He loves righteousness and hates wickedness. That's where the anointing of gladness abides. He does see those who are looking for ways to stay in the mud (sin) and those who are trying to get out (righteousness). When we experience the Bridegroom's joy and pleasure in a very personal way, it is the greatest motivation for obedience. Loving and voluntary obedience to God is our love for Him. Voluntary obedience is where we go from duty to delight; we go from I must to I desire. We go from absolute boredom to absolute fascination. We behold a happy God who enjoys breaking out with the most unique smile you have ever seen. Hallelujah!

It is wrong ideas about God's personality that gets in the way with your relationship with Him. What God wrote on paper He wants you to write it in your heart and soul. He wants you to be convinced of His gladness and delight in you. Is it really worth believing and living in the opposite mindset? Think of how many years are being wasted by thinking that God is constantly disappointed in you. Just look at the life of King David. He wasn't perfect, and definitely had his struggles and issues in his life, but he chose to rise above the negativity. Listen to his testimony of God's sheer delight over his life that brought him deliverance.

 *He also brought me out into a broad place; <u>He delivered me because He delighted in me</u>.*

Psalm 18:19

5. The Bridegroom God Yearns for Intimacy With Us

The fifth and last aspect of discovering Jesus as a Bridegroom is knowing that He yearns for intimacy with us. I believe one of the hardest things we will struggle with is learning to carve out time in our daily calendar and spend time with Jesus, the Bridegroom God. We have so many things that get in the way. Our schedules seem to fill up so fast, and we have many demands with our time. How often have you found yourself saying: I just don't have time to get alone with God? I'm just too busy. Now do you actually buy into that lie? The problem doesn't lie in a lack of time but a lack of priority. It's actually a lack of desire because whatever you desire and want in life that you will pursue. We read the passage earlier in Psalm 27:4 which says; *one thing I have desired of the Lord that will I seek*...Do you notice the words "desired" and "seek?" When you desire something you really want and it's meaningful to you, you will pursue it, and go after it. The more you value something, the more you protect it. No one can change your lifestyle and schedule, not even your spouse or pastor. You must be the one who makes the decision to make a radical change in your schedule and give the Lord first priority. You must be the one who acknowledges that you are bankrupt without having the living flame of love inside your heart. This definitely includes me as well.

I am convinced that a life of intimacy is all about "first love." I believe this is what the Holy Spirit is highlighting in a very specific and focused way. All of heaven is shouting forth like a trumpet: return to your first love.

 *Nevertheless I have this against you, that you have left your first love.*

Revelation 2:4

One of the characteristics of first love is the desire to be as close to the Beloved as possible. We can't preach to others about intimacy and first love if it doesn't grab us in such a way, that anything less makes us miserable. We cannot put the great commission before the great commandment. Burnout is inevitable if we do.

Jesus, the Bridegroom, is filled with extravagant passion for us. Every other human love fades into nothingness. There is no one who can love like Him. It is why He yearns for our love and desires to take complete possession of us. He will not be satisfied until we give ourselves wholly unto Him. Divided love is of so little value to Him. He will not enter into a bond of love with such a soul. Jesus has the right to make such a claim upon our love and intimacy because there is no One so full of glory and so full of royal beauty as Him. He knows what He can bestow with His love. He knows how happy He can make a human soul. That is why He has a thousand times more right than any earthly bridegroom to say, "give me everything; give me your first love."

Intimacy with the Bridegroom God is our highest calling. There is absolutely nothing more important in our lives than abiding in nearness and closeness to the heart of God. Wholehearted love is within our reach. Remember, He first loved us. He first pursued us. **He first planted the seed of passion's fire inside us.** We have been empowered to become lovers of God who will live a lifestyle of intimacy and first love. It's time to have a big Yes and go for it!

 *In this is love, not that we loved God, but that He loved us and sent His Son to be the propitiation for our sins.*

1 John 4:10

How to Nourish Intimacy with the Bridegroom God

The Bridegroom message and foundation is a call to intimacy with Jesus. Intimacy with God is the easiest thing to do. You don't have to have a degree to get alone with God. Anyone can do it. But it's also one of the greatest challenges we will face. This passionate love between Jesus and His bride must be continually nourished in order to have a vibrant and dynamic relationship with Him. Our heart is like a garden, and if we don't tend and nourish our garden, then our heart will start drying up. Weeds will start taking root and destroy the garden. But the good news is we do love the Lord and will say yes to a life of intimacy with Him. We will take our relationship seriously and faithfully cultivate the garden of our heart. We do it because we love Him. The fact we love someone we have never seen before shouts volumes of passionate love. We declare to heaven that we are lovers of God!

 *And though you have not seen Him, you love Him, and though you do not see Him now, but believe in Him, you greatly rejoice with joy inexpressible and full of glory, obtaining as the outcome of your faith the salvation of your souls.*

1 Peter 1:8-9 (NASB)

Here are some simple steps of how to practice nourishing intimacy and bridal love with the Bridegroom God. Don't rush over them, but take some quality time to let them grab hold of you.

1 **To nourish intimacy with the Bridegroom, we need to practice the love of Jesus by uttering His name and adoring Him.** Adoration is powerful! It's the words "I love you" that deeply move His heart. When is the last time you said out loud or whispered; "Jesus, I love you?" When we declare the name of Jesus, His glory begins to shine on us. When we speak of our Beloved often, we will be inflamed with His fiery love. His name is called "Wonderful Counselor, Mighty God, Everlasting Father, Prince of peace." (see Isaiah 9:6)

2 **To nourish intimacy with the Bridegroom, we need to**

spend quality time in worship and in the Word of God. The International House of Prayer of Kansas City calls it "worship with the Word." It's awesome to actually focus on a key passage and develop it with prophetic singers that go deep together as a team. When I was a prayer leader at IHOPKC, I really enjoyed flowing with the prophetic singers in "harp & bowl" worship. It's time to get in the Word of God and become students of God's passionate desire and emotions for us. When I get alone with God to have intimacy with Him, I like playing anointed worship music in the background while reading and praying the scriptures out loud. One song I have played hundreds of times that moves my heart and never gets old is called "No other." The album is <u>I will lift my hands</u> by Vineyard, and sung by David Ruis. This song is found in Psalm 87:7 and is the fulfillment of passion for Jesus. Go ahead and play it while you sing the Word of God and worship. The goal as you sing the Word is to start feeling what you're reading on paper. You don't have to have a good voice to do it. When you sing the Word, you don't use your mind but your spirit. The Holy Spirit takes the information from your mind right to your spirit. I encourage you to try it. It was Paul the Apostle who encourages us to sing the Word of God with our understanding.

 *What is the conclusion then? I will pray with the spirit, and I will also pray with the understanding. I will sing with the spirit, and I will also sing with the understanding.*

1 Corinthians 14:15

Speaking to one another in psalms and hymns and spiritual songs, singing and making melody in your heart to the Lord.

Ephesians 5:19

3   **To nourish intimacy with the Bridegroom, we need to do everything "for His name's sake."** We are more interested in finding ways to make God happy than making ourselves happy. It is the words "for you" that have power. They are like wings transporting us to the One we love. As we do things for His name's sake, it makes difficult tasks easy. Your bridal love will be set aflame when you do everything together all day long with Jesus, the Bridegroom God. Do the smallest things with Him and for His name's sake.

4   **To nourish intimacy with the Bridegroom, we need to meditate upon the sufferings of Christ and His resurrection power.** Jesus is the Man of sorrows. In heaven, He bears the marks and wounds on His hands and feet and appears as the Lamb who was slain for the nations of the earth (see Revelation 5:6). Jesus was wounded for love. The bloody crucifixion is the greatest proof of His passionate love. Because He was resurrected in power, so we will be resurrected one glorious day. We will be given authority over the nations. Forever thankful, forever pondering over and over the suffering and resurrection of Jesus, the Bridegroom God.

5   **To nourish intimacy with the Bridegroom, we need to long and anticipate for our Lover to come back to the earth.** It's called the second coming of Christ. When we no longer expect and look forward to His second coming, the flame of our love will grow dim. When our thoughts center on Him coming on the clouds of heaven, we will speak and sing of it often. This will bring Him closer to our heart, and our love will increase. The Bridegroom God is coming back on a gorgeous white stallion, and His eyes are pictured as liquid fire. His voice sounds like the powerful Niagara Falls in Canada. His face is shining brighter than the sun at midday (see Revelation 19:11-16).

Jesus is coming for a bridal partner to rule and reign with Him forever. Intimacy and reigning with Jesus on the earth in close partnership is the message of Jesus, the Bridegroom God. It's time to discover it!

CHAPTER 2
The Beauty of the Bride

Do you believe you are the bride of Christ? Do you see yourself as beautiful before the Bridegroom God? It's your spiritual identity as God's cherished bride!

The bride of Christ is a position of privilege and honor. The revelation of the beauty of the bride will be poured out upon the earth like never before. At the core of the message which showcases the Father's glory, is how Jesus could take former enemies and transform them into voluntary lovers without violating their free will. **These voluntary lovers will be shining in radiant beauty and sitting on the throne of God with Jesus**. They will rule in divine partnership and authority with Him. That's amazing, former enemies of God now enthroned with the King of the universe.

 *Those who are victorious will sit with me on my throne, just as I was victorious and sat with my Father on his throne.*

Revelation 3:21

I don't know about you, but this was a big challenge to see myself as the bride, of Christ. And to take it even further, the greater challenge was to see myself beautiful in God's eyes. When I think of a bride, I'm thinking of a woman in a beautiful white wedding dress. But after studying scripture, I discovered that the bride is not about gender, it's about divine privilege from the heart of God. It is by faith we receive the truth of what Jesus says about us as His beautiful bride.

Labels don't define you, titles don't define you, being rich or poor doesn't define you, and your position at your job doesn't define you. Only God Himself defines you. He defines you not by what you have done or accomplished but what He has done for you. Being Jesus beautiful bride is your destiny. It's who you will be forever in His eyes.

There are so many passages that reveal the beauty of the bride, especially in the Song of Solomon and Psalm 45, but the passage I want to focus on is found in Revelation 21. I believe this chapter gives us the most profound revelation and perfect picture of the beauty of the bride.

The Perfect Picture of the Bride

> *Then I, John, saw the holy city, New Jerusalem, coming down out of heaven from God, prepared as a bride adorned for her husband.... Then one of the seven angels who had the seven bowls filled with the seven last plagues came to me and talked with me, saying, "<u>Come, I will show you the bride, the Lamb's wife</u>." And he carried me away in the Spirit to a great and high mountain, and showed me the great city, the holy Jerusalem, descending out of heaven from God, having the glory of God. Her light was like a most precious stone, like a jasper stone, clear as crystal. Also she had a great and high wall with twelve gates, and twelve angels at the gates, and names written on them, which are the names of the twelve tribes of the children of Israel. There were three*

gates on each side—east, north, south, and west. The wall of the city had twelve foundation stones, and on them were written the names of the twelve apostles of the Lamb. The angel who talked to me held in his hand a gold measuring stick to measure the city, its gates, and its wall. When he measured it, he found it was a square, as wide as it was long. In fact, its length and width and height were each 1,400 miles. Then he measured the walls and found them to be 216 feet thick (according to the human standard used by the angel). The wall was made of jasper, and the city was pure gold, as clear as glass. The wall of the city was built on foundation stones inlaid with twelve precious stones: the first was jasper, the second sapphire, the third agate, the fourth emerald, the fifth onyx, the sixth carnelian, the seventh chrysolite, the eighth beryl, the ninth topaz, the tenth chrysoprase, the eleventh jacinth, the twelfth amethyst. The twelve gates were made of pearls—each gate from a single pearl! And the main street was pure gold, as clear as glass. I saw no temple in the city, for the Lord God Almighty and the Lamb are its temple. And the city has no need of sun or moon, for the glory of God illuminates the city, and the Lamb is its light. The nations will walk in its light, and the kings of the world will enter the city in all their glory. Its gates will never be closed at the end of day because there is no night there. And all the nations will bring their glory and honor into the city. Nothing evil will be allowed to enter, nor anyone who practices shameful idolatry and dishonesty—but only those whose names are written in the Lamb's Book of Life.

Revelation 21:2, 9-27

One of the seven angels that brought destruction to the earth brings John the Apostle a vision as he's carried away in the spirit to a great and high mountain, and sees the bride of Christ. What a stunning sight to behold. The New Jerusalem is the perfect picture of the bride. She is shining in radiant splendor and has the glory of God upon her. Beloved, this is who you are and where you are headed in your journey as Jesus' bride.

The New Jerusalem will be the capital of the entire universe. The writer of Hebrews calls it "heavenly Jerusalem." The New Jerusalem is a very real city that will actually come down to the earth in the future. Heaven is God's current dwelling place, yet the earth is destined to become His future home. What was Jesus' prayer? *"your kingdom come your will be done, on earth as it is in heaven."* The glory of God is there, and the glory and honor of kings and nations will be there. At the very core of the eternal city is the throne and the Lamb.

After these things I looked, and behold, a great multitude which no one could number, of all nations, tribes, peoples, and tongues, standing before the throne and before the Lamb, clothed with white robes, with palm branches in their hands.

Revelation 7:9

The New Jerusalem is considered a huge cube-shaped city about fifteen hundred miles in length, width, and height. It can house billions of people. It's designed with pure gold, clear as crystal-like glass. The construction of the wall is made of jasper which is my favorite diamond. The Jasper stone is the first stone of the foundation of the city. The street of the city is made of pure gold, like crystal clear glass. The foundations of the wall are adorned with twelve sparkling gems. These unique diamonds are designed to reflect the glory of God in a spectrum of brilliant color. The wall in the Holy City is estimated to be two hundred and sixteen feet thick. The gates to the city are made of a single pearl. Every gate will be one pearl which is big enough to cover the gateway to the city. These pearls will be larger than people. The streets are paved with the finest gold. The light of the city will be shining through with dazzling beauty. **It's a bright crystal palace full of dazzling splendor.** There is no moon or sun, but the glory of God illuminates it. There is a pure river clear as crystal flowing from the throne and the Lamb. It is not a pond or lake, it's a river. It has a destination. The river doesn't just run over you but it runs through you. It flows right down the middle of the city with the tree of life on both sides of the river. This river is undefiled and has supernatural life flowing in it, just like the leaves of the tree which brings healing to the nations. I believe much healing will take place between different countries. They will all be united as one before the Lamb. There is no sickness, no disease, no death and no more weeping or tears in the eternal city. The bride will have physical bodies that never age or decay. No more back and shoulder pain, yeah God!

Maybe it sounds too good to be true. Maybe you're saying it's only for the most elite and spiritual person. But let's look at what the scriptures say.

But now they desire a better, that is, a heavenly country. Therefore God is not ashamed to be called their God, <u>for He has prepared a city for them</u>.
Hebrews 11:16

This glorious city has already been prepared just for you as God's beloved. You are His beautiful bride pictured as the New Jerusalem coming down out of heaven. When you see the unmistakable beauty of the New Jerusalem, you are seeing a reflection of yourself as the bride of Christ. It's the perfect picture of the bride!

God will move His headquarters to the new earth and will literally take up His residency in the New Jerusalem. We simply don't have the capacity to comprehend the significance of living in an economy where God Himself exists. Can you just imagine the view from your mansion overlooking the Holy City and extending as far as the eye can see from an elevation of fifteen hundred miles? It is fifteen hundred miles full of dazzling fire and pure glory. This is where you are headed in your journey with God. You will have access to the city, walking with your Beloved down the streets of gold through a sea of fifteen hundred miles of radiant beauty. You will enter the corridor of glory as a prepared bride, who is adorned for your Husband.

 *Then I, John, saw the holy city, New Jerusalem, coming down out of heaven from God, prepared as a bride adorned for her husband.*

Revelation 21:2

The Holy City has no darkness. No devil. No evil. No terrorists. No temptation. No corruption. No sin. The Light will shine through the city as lightings and peals of thunder explode from the throne. A beautiful emerald (green) rainbow fully encircles the throne, which shouts and trumpets the mercy of God. The meek will rule and reign in supreme power and authority on the earth. It is certain that God Himself will make all things new.

 *Then He who sat on the throne said, "Behold, I make all things new." And He said to me, "Write, for these words are true and faithful."*

Revelation 21:5

I think one of the big mistakes we make is to separate the New Jerusalem and the bride of Christ. To make it simple the New Jerusalem is a real city and is a perfect picture of the bride, and the bride is a beautiful picture of the New Jerusalem descending out of heaven to the earth. The city and the bride are one!

The Bride Shining like a Jasper Diamond

In Revelation 4, we have a heavenly description of God the Father sitting on His throne. He is shining in the pure light like a jasper diamond. This stone is clear as crystal. It's full of dazzling glory and splendor. What a stunning sight to behold: God is shining like a jasper diamond!

And He who sat there was like a jasper and a sardius stone in appearance; and there was a rainbow around the throne, in appearance like an emerald.
Revelation 4:3

In Revelation 21, we now have a beautiful picture of the bride shining like a jasper diamond.

Then one of the seven angels who had the seven bowls filled with the seven last plagues came to me and talked with me, saying, "Come, I will show you the bride, the Lamb's wife." And he carried me away in the Spirit to a great and high mountain, and showed me the great city, the holy Jerusalem, descending out of heaven from God, having the glory of God. <u>Her light was like a most precious stone, like a jasper stone, clear as crystal.</u>
Revelation 21:9-11

It is one thing for God to be shining in the radiant light like a jasper diamond, but we as the bride are also shining forth in the radiant light like a jasper diamond. **We shine just like our Father!** It's the beauty of who you are at its highest place. The last portion of the passage we just read says; *Her light was like a precious stone, like a jasper stone, clear as crystal.* Your light shines and sparkles like the jasper diamond. It's not just the New Jerusalem that's shining in glory, but you as the bride are shining in full glory as well. What a contrast there is between the earthly city represented as a prostitute and the heavenly city as a bride. It's the tale of two cities: the harlot and the bride.

Lovely in the Eyes of the King

I want to shift gears as we conclude on the beauty of the bride. Let's peer into Song of Solomon 1 and discover how lovely we are in the eyes of the Bridegroom King.

Just as the Bridegroom God sees your beauty and loveliness before Him, so He wants you to see it and feel it as well. He wants you anchored and convinced that you are His stunning workmanship before the throne of God. As the bride of Christ, you cannot afford to live without this revelation of being lovely before God. Remember, Revelation 21 is the perfect picture of the bride. It will be your confidence all throughout your journey in the wilderness. Even when you are at the lowest place in your life, you can still say with confidence before heaven: I am lovely in His eyes!

 *I am dark, but lovely,* O daughters of Jerusalem, Like the tents of Kedar, Like the curtains of Solomon.

Song of Solomon 1:5

In Song of Solomon 1, the Shulamite testifies to the Daughters of Jerusalem that she is lovely. She already knew that she was dark and sinful. Sadly, this is the only image many believers have of themselves. But it doesn't have to be that way. Absolute confidence will arise inside you when you start believing and feeling just a little bit of how beautiful and captivating you are to God's heart.

The Shulamite was being confronted in her belief system about her being lovely to the King. Have you ever thought of yourself being lovely to God? I know for me I didn't have too much problem seeing the Lord as being beautiful in heaven, but for me to be lovely in the eyes of the King, I don't think so. But over time as I began to study, meditate and sing the Word of God of my beauty in Him, I began to have a positive mindset, a beauty focus that would change my life completely. I got sick in tired of always being dark and negative focused, living in guilt and condemnation. Sometimes you need to come to a place where you are sick and tired of being sick and tired. When you look at others, is it easier to see the positive things or negative things in them? It will help show you where your mindset and belief system stands.

In Psalm 45, we have a contemplation of the Sons of Korah, writing a song of love. Listen to the bold prophetic declaration of the beauty of the bride, and how the King portrays her. Spend some time camping out in this amazing passage.

> *The royal daughter is all glorious within the palace; Her clothing is woven with gold. She shall be brought to the King in robes of many colors; The virgins, her companions who follow her, shall be brought to You. With gladness and rejoicing they shall be brought;They shall enter the King's palace.*
>
> Psalm 45:13-15

Is it possible to feel confident of being lovely to the King knowing that we are dark inside? This is where we face our identity crisis. I believe it is possible. Yes, we are dark and sinful, but that's not the end of our story. We are lovely as well. We see where the Jasper God is taking us in Revelation 21. Listen to what Paul the Apostle says about the bride of Christ.

> *But we have this treasure in earthen vessels, that the excellence of the power may be of God and not of us.*
>
> 2 Corinthians 4:7

Do you believe there is a treasure inside you? Do you see the treasure or do you only see the earthen vessel? What if God was to give you a radiant idea of who you really are in His eyes. What if you could see yourself the same way He sees you. You would feel ten feet taller. When you become lovely focused, it takes you out of a negative mindset. You stop living in shame always feeling condemned, and start living with confidence and boldness before heaven.

In your journey to wholehearted love, you are being trained in your belief system to know and feel that you are beautiful and radiant in God's eyes because you have the righteousness of Christ. It's not about your righteousness but His. Because of Jesus' sinless perfection, you can find your identity and beauty in Him. Your loveliness streams from the glorious gift of Christ's righteousness.

> *For He made Him who knew so sin to be sin for us, that we might become the righteousness of God in Him.*
>
> 2 Corinthians 5:21

Our righteousness occurred instantly on the day we were born again. It cannot be improved upon. Every legal hindrance that would keep God from receiving us is removed forever. **The King of glory sees something in you that nobody else sees**. He sees you as a champion because a champion lives in you. He sees the fight in you to resist temptation and darkness. He sees your willing spirit, and that's lovely to Him. It's Christ in you the hope of glory (see Colossians 1:27). When people look at you, they may only see a shepherd boy, but when God looks at you, He sees a king. That's who you are "kings and priests" reigning with Jesus before the glory of heaven.

> *And they sang a new song, saying: "You are worthy to take the scroll, And to open its seals; For You were slain, And have redeemed us to God by Your blood Out of every tribe and tongue and people and nation, And have made us kings and priests to our God; And we shall reign on the earth."*
>
> Revelation 5:9-10

Do you know where your journey in God is taking you? I am here to tell you that you are lovely and spiritually attractive right now to the Bridegroom God. You don't have to gain a smile that you already have. When God looks at you, He doesn't just see all the negative things in your life as others do, but He mostly sees the beautiful and positive things as well. To say it again, you may not see anything in yourself that is desirable at this moment, but God does. Beauty is in the eyes of the beholder!

Do you want to hear something that will blow your mind away? The King of the universe, the One who created all the galaxies from nothing; **He greatly desires your beauty**. It's very personal and profound to Him. He not only desires that you reflect His beauty, but He _greatly_ desires it.

> *So the King will greatly desire your beauty; Because He is your Lord, worship Him.*
>
> Psalm 45:11

CHAPTER 3
The Glory of Loving God

The Pharisees knew the Ten Commandments and the laws of the Pentateuch so well. They were legalists focused on performance and acting like they were more holy than everyone else. They didn't live life from the inside out, and never knew the Son of God in a personal and intimate way.

It was one of the Pharisees, a lawyer, who in Matthew 22 asked Jesus a simple yet profound question, but was also testing Him. I don't think he really understood the significance of what he asked. He says to Jesus: *What is the great commandment in the Law?* In Mark 12:28 it says; *Which is the first commandment of all?*

> *Jesus replied, "'You must love the L<small>ORD</small> your God with all your heart, all your soul, and all your mind.' This is the <u>first</u> and greatest commandment. A second is equally important: 'Love your neighbor as yourself.' The entire law and all the demands of the prophets are based on these two commandments."*
>
> Matthew 22:37-40

There are two very important things that Jesus highlights in His response to the Pharisee. They are directly related to everything going on in our personal lives and are of great significance.

1. The commandment to love Jesus with all your heart, all your soul, and all your mind is to be *FIRST*. It's not second or third. It's the first commandment. There is nothing more important than our heart growing in holy passion for the Son of God. Because Jesus wants to be first in our lives, so we need to put loving Him wholeheartedly first. He will not relent until He has all of us. Do you notice the word "all" in this passage? God is not interested that we love Him fifty percent or even ninety-five percent. He desires and urges us to love Him one hundred percent, with ALL of our heart.

The number one agenda on God's heart is to restore the first commandment to first place. I believe most of the teaching in the body of Christ today is focused upon prosperity and healing. It's why you can be a prophetic voice in our generation that teaches on the first commandment, and the glory of loving God.

I believe the first commandment is all about "first love." We talked about this earlier in chapter one. We do not want to regret not living this lifestyle before heaven. If Jesus is not first in our lives, then who or what is first? Whatever you're putting first, does it offer a lifetime of utter satisfaction and enjoyment? Does it offer a supernatural realm of glory in the midst of chaos? I don't think so. It is time we start putting Jesus first in everything we do because there is none like Him. He deserves our affections first, even before our spouse or children. It's time to return to our first love in a radical way.

> *Nevertheless I have this against you, that you have left your first love.*
>
> Revelation 2:4

Beloved, first love is radical and not passive. It requires an aggressive and holy determination to pursue. We are the ones who left our first love not Him. It never even crossed God's mind to do something like that. His passion and commitment towards His bride will never waiver. His faithfulness and mercy will always be with us.

> *But <u>My faithfulness</u> and <u>My mercy</u> shall be with him, And in My name his horn shall be exalted.*
>
> Psalm 89:24

2. The commandment to love Jesus with all your heart, all your soul, and all your mind is the *GREATEST* in His eyes. This was the other important thing that Jesus highlights in His response to the Pharisee in Matthew 22. Let's read it again.

> *Jesus replied, "'You must love the LORD your God with all your heart, all your soul, and all your mind.' This is the first and <u>greatest</u> commandment. A second is equally important: 'Love your neighbor as yourself.' The entire law and all the demands of the prophets are based on these two commandments.*
>
> Matthew 22:37-40

Not only is this commandment that Jesus is talking about to be first in our lives, but it's to be the greatest as well. I call it the heartbeat of all commands. The highest calling in life is "voluntary love" displayed on the earth. There are three types of obedience in scripture: Disobedience, mandatory obedience, and voluntary obedience. It is the latter one which is most powerful in God's Kingdom and will be richly rewarded. Voluntary obedience to Jesus is the greatest commandment fulfilled.

To obey Jesus means we gladly do what is right in His eyes, not because we have to but because we want to. We choose to love Him with wholehearted obedience, knowing it's the greatest commandment from His heart. That's how Jesus describes true love for Him. I would simply call it loving obedience.

> *If you love Me, keep My commandments.*
>
> John 14:15

Many believers try to find out how much they can get away with by engaging in secret sin but still wanting to love God. You cannot love Jesus and still be hanging out in the spirit of darkness. The bible says; *God is light and in Him is no darkness at all* (see 1 John 1:5). The question we must ask the Lord is: how deep can I be abandoned to you? That question and prayer is what moves the heart of God. He applauds it as GREAT to Him.

Love cannot be passive. Love is spiritually violent. We all want something from God, but do we ever ask Him what He wants from us? The God of the universe has everything He needs, yet is looking for something from us. What is it He wants? He desires wholehearted abandonment to His leadership; living in the glory of loving Him as our greatest pursuit we can achieve. He wants us to resist the desires of our flesh, and live a life in the Spirit because we love God. That is the first and great commandment Jesus treasures most. It is loving Him with all our heart, all our soul, and all our mind.

Maybe you're asking why does Jesus want us to love Him with all of our heart? That's the great question of the ages. Let me give you a few reasons why He asks this supreme request.

Jesus wants us to love Him with all of our heart because He loves us with all His heart. That's powerful. If that doesn't motivate us to obey Him out of love I don't know what will. Let's look again at the passage which is the premise for my book.

> *We love Him because He first loved us.*
> John 4:19

Jesus holds nothing back in fully loving us. He takes our relationship with Him as more important than anything. It is not a game. It's not something we can take lightly. He first pursued us even when we never pursued Him. He first sacrificed Himself while we never sacrificed anything. I think it's a good time to say thank you, Jesus, for first loving me. Thank you for being so good to me. I set my heart to love You with all my heart because You love me with all Your heart.

Jesus wants us to love Him with all of our heart because of the eternal rewards, we will reap. The Bible is full of rewards. It's one of God's greatest motivations to awaken our heart for Him. Instead of me giving you some bible passages of rewards which I encourage you to study, I want you to focus on the highest and primary reward in scripture. It's God Himself!

> *After these things the word of the* LORD *came to Abram in a vision, saying, "Do not be afraid, Abram. I am your shield, <u>your exceedingly great reward.</u>"*
> Genesis 15:1

Jesus wants us to love Him with all of our heart for the sake of the world. Because God so loves the world, He wants us to partner with Him by imitating His life and character to the nations. When the first commandment is first in our lives, then the second commandment flows perfectly through us. We receive love and give that love away. That's called divine order!

Jesus wants our light to shine in a dark world. We are His voice to the lost and hurting. We have the ability from heaven to impart life and salvation to others. Jesus has commissioned us to make disciples of all nations. It's called the great commission.

> *And Jesus came and spoke to them, saying, "All authority has been given to Me in heaven and on earth. Go therefore and make disciples of all the nations, baptizing them in the name of the Father and of the Son and of the Holy Spirit, teaching them to observe all things that I have commanded you; and lo, I am with you always, even to the end of the age." Amen.*
> Matthew 28:18-20

Loving Jesus without Offense

I believe there are many ways we prove our love for Jesus. If I was to pick one word or one reality that truly demonstrates our love for God it would be "offense." To love Jesus with all of our heart means we are not offended at His leadership in spite of the difficult and painful circumstances we face. That is the glory of loving God. Listen to what Jesus says in Luke 7.

> *And blessed is he who is not offended because of Me.*
>
> Luke 7:23

The offense occurs when we don't understand what God is doing in our lives. When our timing doesn't match His timing, we get easily offended. When God doesn't give us what we prayed for we are offended by Him. When we go through long periods of suffering, we get mad at God and offended because we don't think He's involved or paying attention to us. We must choose to love Jesus in the midst of adversity no matter how difficult it gets. So many believers go through life trying to avoid pain. But we must embrace it knowing that God is removing offense in our lives; He's removing everything that hinders love. He's preparing and making us ready for the great wedding day – the marriage of the Lamb. Let's pray this short, yet revolutionary prayer together as the body of Christ. **Jesus, would you do something in me that changes everything?** Amen!

I don't think we fully understand "why" the Lord allows pain and suffering in our lives. Otherwise, we wouldn't be easily offended. Suffering is a gift from God's heart. It is not a waste of time or a mistake. It doesn't mean God is mad at you or trying to pick on you. There is a divine purpose when Jesus takes these jars of clay and transforms them into something beautiful and precious. There is something bigger going on in your life than you think. You are being prepared for something great, something profound. Your being trained in the wilderness to not only prove your love for God by not being offended at Him but to be entrusted with authority and power in your divine calling. It's time to bounce back from defeat. When you love Jesus through the tribulations, He receives all the glory, and you become more like Him. Your love for God is bigger than you think. It has eternal implications. There is a supernatural realm of glory that you can walk in when loving Jesus becomes first, and it's the greatest reality in your life. It is the beauty of loving God. It's glory that you will inherit and possess in the eternal city.

> *For I consider that the sufferings of this present time are not worthy to be compared with the glory which shall be revealed in us.*
>
> Romans 8:18

Three Most Powerful Words to God's Heart

There is no better way to conclude this chapter by sharing with you the three most powerful words you can utter to Jesus, the Bridegroom God. It's a huge part of our journey of living in the glory of loving God in the first commandment. Throughout my journey with the Lord I have prayed for many different things and said many things to Him, but I believe the most powerful words I have said to Him is "I love you."

When speaking these words to God, it must be a reality and come straight from the heart. You say it because you really mean it. When was the last time you spoke or whispered these three beautiful words to Jesus? "I love you." Ponder over that question.

If you haven't spoken those words in a while, it reveals you have drifted from your first love. You're probably living in mandatory obedience and not voluntary obedience. Maybe outwardly, people look at you and think you're so happy, but deep inside you are miserable, and you know it. Don't get too discouraged; I have been there before. Be thankful you see where you really stand, and start receiving the truth of what God thinks and feels about you, and press into God's heart. Repent and break off the spirit of condemnation. It doesn't come from Him. Don't be so hard on yourself because Jesus is not that way towards you. Remember, passion for Jesus comes from discovering His passion for you. It's not about your commitment to Him but His commitment to you.

Start declaring to heaven that you are a lover of God. I like what Mike Bickle says about being a lover of God. He says; "we are not sinners struggling to love God, but are lovers of God who struggle with sin." Let's look at the passage again in 1 Peter 1:8-9. Say it right now; Jesus, I love you. I really love you. I love you because you first loved me. Say this phrase every day: "I am loved, and I'm a lover, this is who I am, and this is what I do." You will enter into the glory of loving God. You are a lover of God!

> *And though you have not seen Him, you love Him, and though you do not see Him now, but believe in Him, you greatly rejoice with joy inexpressible and full of glory, obtaining as the outcome of your faith the salvation of your souls.*
>
> 1 Peter 1:8-9 (NASB)

CHAPTER 4
The Seven Longings of the Bridal Paradigm

I believe one of the greatest blessings we as God's beloved have received is the power of longing, the power to be deeply moved on the inside. It's a gift from His heart. What would life be like without having the ability to long and yearn for something? What would it be like to not be able to feel any emotions within us? Life would be miserable.

Longing is directly connected to our emotions. It's the ability to feel, yearn, and desire something meaningful. The greatest longing we can have is the longing to abide in the presence of Jesus all the days of our lives.

> *How lovely is Your tabernacle, O LORD of hosts! My soul longs, yes, even faints For the courts of the LORD; My heart and my flesh cry out for the living God.*
> Psalm 84:1-2

We all have different longings in our journey with God. What would be your top seven longings in order that you want to see come to pass? Before reading on, go ahead and write them down and start praying over them in a focused way.

I want to look at seven longings of the bridal paradigm. They are very real and within reach of every one of us. The bridal paradigm simply means we see ourselves as Jesus' bride to the Bridegroom God. It is the revelation of God's beauty and our beauty before Him. When we enter the bridal paradigm, we enter into the divine romance of the gospel. Let's pray and meditate on these seven longings to cultivate passion for Jesus.

1. The first longing of the bridal paradigm is the longing to know that we are enjoyed by God. This is a powerful craving we received the day we got born again. Who wants to feel that you're just a burden or disappointment to God? There is unending enjoyment and pleasure in His presence.

> *You will show me the path of life; <u>In Your presence is fullness of joy</u>; At Your right hand are pleasures forevermore.*
>
> Psalm 16:11

We can imagine that God will enjoy us when we are in heaven, but we can't imagine Him enjoying us in our daily lives upon the earth. The idea that God can enjoy us even if we are spiritually immature is unthinkable. But the truth is God does enjoy us as His bride. That's why He died in utter agony at Golgotha. When we feel enjoyed by the Lord, it releases power and confidence inside of us. **The joy of the Lord breaks off depression.** It removes shame and condemnation and causes us to run towards God and not away from Him.

How does God feel most of the time as He peers down from His holy throne? This question is one of the most important questions we need to ask in our walk with the Lord. It reveals where we really stand in our identity as a believer. Without feeling God's delight and enjoyment over us, we become discouraged, never feeling like we measure up to please Him. It's not about trying harder but enjoying more. Even Jesus needed to hear from His Father how He felt over Him. This was before His public ministry and any miracles performed. If the Son of God needed to hear and feel the enjoyment of His Father over His life, how much more do we need to hear it?

> *And suddenly a voice came from heaven, saying, "This is My beloved Son, in whom I am well pleased."*
>
> Matthew 3:17

Until you are convinced that the happiest person in the world is God Himself, then it will be a constant struggle to embrace the revelation of God's enjoyment over your life. Jesus has been glad for billions of years and will always be glad, overflowing with joy. It flows right from His dwelling place.

> *Splendor and majesty are before him; strength and joy are in his dwelling place.*
>
> 1 Chronicles 16:27 (NIV)

Do you believe that God is rejoicing over you with a big smile right now? Do you believe He's singing over you with joy as His sons and daughters? If you're having a hard time accepting this reality, then I encourage you to get alone with God and let Him quiet you with His love. His outrageous mercy will remove any hindrance. If we behold an angry God, we will become an angry person. If we behold a God who is always disappointed in us, we will live in constant disappointment. If we behold a sad God, we will live in perpetual sadness. But if we behold a happy God who rejoices over us, we will live with a happy heart on the inside. Where is your focus? That's the key!

I want to say it again and make clear that God really enjoys us as His bride, but it doesn't mean that He agrees with everything we do. Whenever we are convicted of our sins, it simply means that He does not want us living at a distance from Him. He is getting everything out of the way so we can have a close and abiding relationship with Him. Let's start thanking the Lord by declaring and singing out loud that God is happy with us. He does enjoy us and will satisfy the longing to know it and feel it. Knowing we are enjoyed by God brings freedom and deliverance in our lives. This was King David's testimony: delight equals deliverance.

> *He also brought me out into a broad place; <u>He delivered me because He delighted in me.</u>*
>
> Psalm 18:19

2. The second longing of the bridal paradigm is the longing to be fascinated. The power to be deeply moved within is something we all long for. Without having a sense of awe and fascination of God's heart we live spiritually bored. Do you realize that God is the author of pleasure and marvel? It was His idea that the ones He created would have the capacity to be fascinated in their spirit. We must believe and get it in our thought life that there is a fascination in God to experience, so we can live exhilarated in our walk with Jesus. We can't repent for our desire and longing to be captivated by God's majesty in a real and authentic way. Remember, the Lord is the author of spiritual pleasure. It's not just pleasure, but it's a river of pleasure!

> *They are abundantly satisfied with the fullness of Your house, <u>And You give them drink from the river of Your pleasures</u>. For with You is the fountain of life; In Your light we see light.*
>
> Psalm 36:8-9

The secular industry has targeted this area in a very powerful way. You must not allow yourself to be allured by the spirit of this age. Whether you realize it or not, you will either be fascinated by the Spirit of God or the spirit of this world. It's your choice. No matter who you are or what your background is, you have a deep void inside you. It's a God-shaped vacuum. Will you pursue pleasure in God or pleasure in this world? The pleasure found in the world is only a temporary pleasure and leads to ultimate destruction. It doesn't have the anointing of heaven upon it. Have you ever thought about why we sin? Because it produces immediate pleasure and gives a physical and emotional rush. We don't sin out of obligation. We sin because we like the immediate pleasure it brings.

The power of temptation rests on a deceptive promise that sin will bring more satisfaction than living for God. The scriptures call it "the deceitfulness of sin." The secret to conquering the power of sin is satisfaction and fascination with God. John Piper says; "sin is what you do when you're not satisfied in your relationship with Jesus." I will never forget what Sam Storms, who was one of the Bible teachers at Grace Training Centre with Mike Bickle just before IHOPKC was birthed. He said; "You minimize sin by maximizing the pleasures of God."

I believe there are many believers who are serving a God who is emotionless or distant in their walk with Him. It's why they are spiritually bored and dull. It's time to pray and seek the Lord's heart for a fresh revelation of His majesty, so we can become fascinated and exhilarated. Just like the thrill of going on a fast and wild roller coaster ride, so we can be thrilled and fascinated with the nature of God's personality. **We must have a vision for divine entertainment in God**. It's time we see the smile of His majesty in a deep and personal way that radically impacts and changes us.

It is the Holy Spirit who escorts us on a treasure hunt into the majesty of Jesus. I believe the majesty realm of God is where we become most fascinated. In Ezekiel 1, we have an amazing passage describing the glory of the God-Man Jesus Himself. The prophet gazed far into the heavens and saw a Man upon the throne full of dazzling glory. His appearance was like a sapphire stone (deep blue), and He looked like glowing metal. He was consumed with the appearance of fire all around. The word appearance is mentioned nine times in just three verses. Ezekiel was probably thinking to himself; how could a human being be sitting at the top of God's empire? Absolutely stunning!

> *And above the firmament (sea of glass) over their heads was the likeness of a throne, in appearance like a sapphire stone; on the likeness of the throne was a likeness with the appearance of a man high above it. Also from the appearance of His waist and upward I saw, as it were, the color of amber (glowing metal) with the appearance of fire all around within it; and from the appearance of His waist and downward I saw, as it were, the appearance of fire with brightness all around. Like the appearance of a rainbow in a cloud on a rainy day, so was the appearance of the brightness all around it. This was the appearance of the likeness of the glory of the LORD.*
>
> Ezekiel 1:26-28

3. The third longing of the bridal paradigm is the longing to feel beautiful. Just as most human beings have a desire to look beautiful or handsome in physical appearance, so we as Jesus' bride have a desire and need to feel beautiful spiritually. It is one thing to **know** you are lovely to God, but it's a whole different reality to **feel** beautiful before Him. When you feel beautiful in your spirit, it breaks off all shame and condemnation. Our beauty and loveliness come from the beauty of Jesus Himself. The beauty that He possesses is the beauty that He imparts.

In Song of Solomon 4, the Bridegroom God speaks a radical declaration of the bride's beauty, telling her she has dove's eyes before Him. A dove is very pure. They mate for life and are incredibly loyal to each other. Beloved, the Lord speaks this powerful truth over us of who we are to Him. We are like dove's who are pure in heart, and remain loyal to the Lord, and loyal to each other. Our beauty and purity are hidden from the eyes of the world.

> *Behold, you are fair, my love! Behold, you are fair! <u>You have dove's eyes behind your veil.</u> Your hair is like a flock of goats, going down from Mount Gilead.*
>
> Song of Solomon 4:1

4. The fourth longing of the bridal paradigm is the longing to be great and successful. We don't need to feel guilty because we have a longing and desire to be great and successful in our Christian journey, as long as we are pursuing it in the right way. The longing for success is all about being great before the Lord and not man. We live under the audience of one. There is nothing wrong with wanting to be successful in the marketplace. I just spent the last five years working in the marketplace and had a strong drive to be successful. Who wants to fail? My pursuit of success was before heaven and not before any manager or supervisor.

God defines success entirely different than the world does. Success is not about what you have obtained in the natural realm but what you have obtained on the inside of you. It doesn't matter what people think about us, even if they think we are popular or have so many Facebook likes. What matters is how the beautiful God evaluates us in His eyes. It's the great evaluation of success in the kingdom of God. It was Jesus who called John the Baptist the greatest man that was ever born.

> *Assuredly, I say to you, among those born of women there has not risen one greater than John the Baptist; but he who is least in the kingdom of heaven is greater than he.*
>
> Matthew 11:11

God left the door open to any believer that desires to be greater and surpass the life of John the Baptist. Do you notice Jesus links greatness to being least in His kingdom? Now that doesn't mean that you're content to sit in the last row in heaven. I want to be as close and near to Jesus and His throne as I can. You should have the same desire for success as well. Being least in God's kingdom is about servanthood; it's modeling the life and character of our Beloved in scripture. Jesus set an example as He washed the feet of the disciples, including Judas who betrayed Him. If you want to rise to the top, then you need to stoop low to the bottom. Servanthood is about serving others and making them great and not yourself. You rejoice when God promotes and exalts other people, even if you don't think they deserve it. It's about living a life of humility and meekness before the eyes of the One upon the throne. It was Jesus who said that the meek would inherit the earth (see Matthew 5:5).

Meekness is power under control. It's restraining yourself with a higher purpose in mind. Jesus demonstrated this during His bloody crucifixion. He could have wiped out all the Roman soldiers who were crucifying Him, but He restrained Himself with a grand purpose of having a spotless bride reigning with Him in divine partnership. Hallelujah!

The Bride is Destined to Reign and Shine

In 1 Samuel 2, it was Hannah who prayed this amazing prayer that will go down in history as one of the greatest. It's one of the main reasons I named my daughter Hannah. I so love and adore my little girl. And I so love and adore my little boy David!

> *The LORD makes poor and makes rich; He brings low and lifts up. He raises the poor from the dust And lifts the beggar from the ash heap, To set them among princes And make them inherit the throne of glory. For the pillars of the earth are the LORD's, And He has set the world upon them.*
>
> 1 Samuel 2:7-8

King David testified that it was God's gentleness that made him great. He was king of Israel for forty successful years. He was great because of God's gentleness to him.

> *You have also given me the shield of Your salvation; Your right hand has held me up, Your gentleness has made me great.*
>
> Psalm 18:35

Not only are we destined to reign forever, but we are destined to shine brightly in a dark world. It's all a part of our spiritual journey to be successful. The bride is destined to be great on that day, the day we see God face to face. It will be our testimony before heaven that we shine like stars in the universe.

> *Do everything without complaining [grumbling] or arguing. Then you will be innocent [blameless] and without any wrong [innocent; pure; harmless], God's children without fault. But you are living with people that are crooked and evil [in the midst of a crooked and perverse generation; among whom you shine like stars in the dark world.*
>
> Philippians 2:15 (EXB)

5. The fifth longing of the bridal paradigm is the longing for intimacy without shame. Because of the finished work of the cross we can be deeply connected with God's heart in intimacy. It seems like I can't get away from the topic of intimacy. It's one of the main themes to develop passion for Jesus. To abide in the power of intimacy, we must not have any shame lingering around. If we always focus on our sins and failures, we will get caught up in the spirit of shame. If we always focus on our past, we will constantly live with guilt and condemnation. **We have to leave the old to see the new**. We focus on who God is transforming us into – a radiant spotless bride.

Beloved, all shame disappears in the presence of Jesus. We have the ability to be as close and intimate to God as we want. It's our choice and, we will never be forced. But there will be a fight and struggle to have constant intimacy with our Beloved. What I have come to realize over the years is that intimacy with God MUST be cultivated.

Cultivating Intimacy with the Bridegroom God

The bride is in training in the wilderness to be entrusted with spiritual authority. She cannot afford to get distracted in her pursuit of holy love and intimacy with the Bridegroom God. It's her highest calling that she must protect and not live without. If she wants her heart to be alive and feel connected with her Lover, then she must fight for the preciousness of intimacy no matter what obstacle or challenge comes her way.

Intimacy in the King's chambers is what prepares us for the battles we face in our lives. It's our destiny to not only have a prayer chamber but a bridal chamber as well. A prayer chamber is where we contend and give out in prayer and intercession. A bridal chamber is where we receive and allow our love tank to be filled by the Bridegroom King. It's the place of adoration. When you come into the bridal chamber, you don't come with a prayer list, but simply love and adore Jesus for who He is and not what He can do for you.

> *Draw me away! We will run after you. The king has brought me into his chambers. We will be glad and rejoice in you. We will remember your love more than wine. Rightly do they love you.*
>
> Song of Solomon 1:4

When we are not cultivating a life of intimacy with God, it shows that we are not connecting with Him on the inside. We're not taking the time to search out and discover His heart beat in the Word of God. Serving Him is less about duty and religion, and more about an intimate relationship with the lover of our soul. We must ask the Holy Spirit to give us a fresh encounter of God's relentless passion for us and set our heart to be intentional to seek and know Him. Ask the Lord to awaken desire for Him, so you can have intimacy without shame, and fulfill that longing within you. Don't be content to live at a distance. Be persistent!

Intimacy with God and wholehearted devotion is not as difficult as we think. It comes from Jesus Himself because He first loved us. But it must be intentional and not just a wish or hope to become a reality. Our deep longing for this lifestyle means we make some radical changes in our lives and pledge our heart to draw near to God, so we can have intimacy without shame. Will you devote and pledge your heart to draw near to God?

> *Their nobles shall be from among them, And their governor shall come from their midst; Then I will cause him to draw near, And he shall approach Me; For who is this who <u>pledged his heart to approach Me</u>?' says the* LORD.
>
> Jeremiah 30:21

6. The sixth longing of the bridal paradigm is the longing to be wholehearted and passionate. We already looked at the glory of loving God and what the first commandment looks like in the first chapter, but I want to share a little more of being wholehearted to God Himself. We need to hear it over and over until this pursuit becomes a reality. How are champions formed to be great? It's by constant repetition.

Jesus strongly desires that His bride be wholehearted and passionate in the midst of compromise, temptation and, total darkness. We have a glorious opportunity to prove our love to the Bridegroom God, as He respects the choices we make. Because Jesus is wholehearted and passionate towards us, He expects the same from us. His plan and strategy are to have a vibrant people on the earth, gladly willing to lay down their lives for His name's sake. If you have nothing to die for, you have nothing to live for. We choose to take up the cross and follow Jesus, our perfect leader.

> *Then He said to them all, If anyone desires to come after Me, let him deny himself, and take up his cross daily, and follow Me. For whoever desires to save his life will lose it, but whoever loses his life for My sake will save it.*
> Luke 9:23-24

God Desires Wholehearted Abandonment

Jesus, the Bridegroom God wants to take complete possession of us, living and contending for His glory. He desires wholehearted abandonment to His wise leadership, even when He doesn't make sense in our lives, or we can't feel His presence. To be abandoned to the Lord simply means we fully relinquish our demands and desires to Him. We must be ready and willing to launch out to the deep seas, and not be content to camp around the shore. That's where faith and adventure come in. We live by faith and not by sight. The stronger your faith in God, the stronger and deeper your abandonment will be.

Maybe heaven seems completely silent, and you can't sense His presence, just accept it knowing Jesus went through the same thing in the Garden of Gethsemane. Silence does not mean that God is not alive upon the throne orchestrating every detail in your life. One thing you must realize, **heaven may be silent at times, but God's heart never stops beating**!

It is Jesus we are living for and not ourselves. Everything that is going on in our lives serves a higher purpose than what we think is right and fair. He has us right where He wants us. He is on the other side of the battle. He knows exactly what He is doing as He gazes from His throne, wanting to show Himself strong and deliver those who are loyal and wholehearted to Him.

> *For the eyes of the LORD run to and fro throughout the whole earth, to show Himself strong on behalf of those whose heart is loyal to Him.*
>
> 2 Chronicles 16:9

There is a purpose beyond ourselves that we might not see in the midst of the storm, but will be clear as daylight when we stand upon the sea of glass like crystal. Every difficulty we have ever gone through is all about Jesus bringing His bride to a place of abandonment to Him. We will agree with His plans and His ways declaring that He is just and true. We need to sign back up by surrendering our lives and returning back to the heart of God. We choose to commit to a life of radical abandonment all the days of our lives. Will you turn back to Jesus with all your heart? Will you make a fresh dedication to be wholeheartedly abandoned to His will? Who knows, maybe He will leave a blessing for you!

> *Now, therefore," says the LORD, "Turn to Me with all your heart, With fasting, with weeping, and with mourning." So rend your heart, and not your garments; Return to the LORD your God, For He is gracious and merciful, Slow to anger, and of great kindness; And He relents from doing harm.* <u>Who</u>

> *knows if He will turn and relent, and leave a blessing behind Him* — *A grain offering and a drink offering For the* LORD *your God?*
>
> Joel 2:12-14

7. The seventh and final longing of the bridal paradigm is the longing to make a deep and lasting impact. Earlier in chapter three, we looked at the greatest commandment in scripture. It was to love God with all your heart, soul and mind. But Jesus goes on in that passage talking about the second commandment. It's loving your neighbor as yourself.

> *And the second is like it: 'You shall love your neighbor as yourself.' On these two commandments hang all the Law and the Prophets.*
>
> Matthew 22:39-40

We simply cannot love God without loving others. It's not possible. Our love for others demonstrates our love for God. I don't have an issue with desiring to love God, but I do have an issue at times desiring to love my neighbor as myself, especially for the difficult people who mistreat me and get to my nerve. Do you have any difficult people in your life that Jesus wants you to love and forgive? That is how we make a deep and lasting impact.

To be able to make an impact on someone we first need to have that desire. We can ask the Holy Spirit to put that desire in us. Making an impact on others will look different for every one of us. For some of us, God has called us to the mission field to preach the gospel to the poor, and lead others to Christ in salvation. For others, it is letting Jesus' light and character shine through us in the marketplace. I don't want to forget about the stay at home moms. You have a great responsibility and challenge to raise your kiddos to love Jesus wholeheartedly. It's important that we go above and beyond to find ways to make an impact on someone. We let our actions preach for us amongst our colleagues at work.

> *Let your light so shine before men, that they may see your good works and glorify your Father in heaven.*
>
> Matthew 5:16

God is not looking for us to preach in front of thousands of people to make an impact and difference in someone's life. It's the simple things like giving someone a hug when they are hurting. It is praying for someone when they are really struggling. It's blessing someone financially when they are barely getting by. It is overcoming evil with good. We need to be sensitive to the leading of the Holy Spirit as to who and what He wants us to do, to make a deep impact upon someone. I love how Jesus defines how to be rewarded before Him as we pursue the longing to make an impact on others. The reward is not found in something huge or dynamic, but in something little and simple; ONLY a cup of cold water. He is easy to please!

> *And whoever gives one of these little ones only a cup of cold water in the name of a disciple, assuredly, I say to you, he shall by no means lose his reward.*
>
> Matthew 10:42

Motivated to Make a Lasting Impact

The Lord has designed His people to make a relevant impact in the lives of others. You can call it "a legacy." If we're not caught up in something bigger than ourselves, then we have missed something special from the throne room of heaven. I believe at the core of making an impact upon others is the power of an unselfish life. We are very selfish by nature, and only the Holy Spirit can change and transform our heart to be unselfish like Him. Just as Jesus stooped down to make others great, so we can do the same.

Beloved, now is the time to ask the beautiful God to give us fresh motivation to make a deep and lasting impact on someone's life. The Lord wants to fulfill that longing within us that He put there. He wants us to share and help those in need, but it will take sacrifice to do it.

> *But do not forget to do good and to share, for with such sacrifices God is well pleased.*
> Hebrews 13:16

CHAPTER 5
The Embrace of Sonship

I believe there are two distinct cries in the end times. I call it "the bridal cry" and the "Abba cry."

The bridal cry can be found in Revelation 22. This distinct cry will be uttered all across the globe to usher in the second coming of Christ.

> *And the Spirit and the bride say, "Come!" And let him who hears say, "Come!" And let him who thirsts come. Whoever desires, let him take the water of life freely.*
>
> Revelation 22:17

At the core of the bridal cry are four pillars (themes) which make up the foundation of the bridal cry.

1. **Intimacy** – We develop a secret life in God's heart.
2. **Cherished** – We are God's favorite one.
3. **Pleasure** – It satisfies the deepest longings in us.
4. **Beauty** – Empowers us to be lovesick for Jesus.

The Abba cry can be found in Romans 8. This distinct cry will restore the Father's heart and sonship back to the hearts of God's children.

> *For as many as are led by the Spirit of God, these are sons of God. For you did not receive the spirit of bondage again to fear, but you received the Spirit of adoption by whom we cry out, "Abba, Father." The Spirit Himself bears witness with our spirit that we are children of God, and if children, then heirs—heirs of God and joint heirs with Christ, if indeed we suffer with Him, that we may also be glorified together.*
>
> Romans 8:14-17

At the core of the Abba cry are four pillars (themes) which make up the foundation of the Abba cry.

1. **Identity** – it forms and fashions who we are.

2. **Embrace** – We receive agape love and feel accepted.

3. **Wholeness** – Brings healing to our soul and emotions.

4. **Maturity** – We are entrusted with spiritual authority.

The Abba cry is all about sonship. It's living and feeling like sons and daughters to the Father heart of God. It doesn't have to do with gender or age but is about a position of privilege in God's kingdom. There is absolutely nothing we did to earn it. I believe the message of sonship is one of the most important messages to be shared in our present generation. It has the power to unlock healing and restoration across the nations of the earth. Sonship is about abiding in the Father's embrace and receiving the deepest love you will ever find. A new paradigm is about to thunder across the earth of true sonship. Get ready!

> *Just as He chose us in Him before the foundation of the world, that we should be holy and without blame before Him in love, having predestined us to adoption as sons by Jesus Christ to Himself, according to the good pleasure of His will.*
>
> Ephesians 1:5

To be chosen and adopted by the Father shows forth His personal affection for you. The Greek word for adoption means "the placing as a son." You have been placed in the most secure and tender hands of the One who holds the universe.

The spiritual crisis on the earth today is fatherlessness. So many believers are not living as if they have a home in the Father's heart, although they call God their Father. I believe that God is going to shake everything that can be shaken. He is exposing the false foundations which we have built in our personal lives and ministry. The crisis of fatherlessness is why the church is experiencing a crisis of identity. Only the revelation of who God the Father is and who we are as His sons can bring true healing and restoration. It is what will heal the spiritual crisis of fatherlessness across the earth.

> *"Remember the Law of Moses, My servant, Which I commanded him in Horeb for all Israel, With the statutes and judgments. Behold, I will send you Elijah the prophet Before the coming of the great and dreadful day of the* LORD. *And he will turn the hearts of the fathers to the children, And the hearts of the children to their fathers, lest I come and strike the earth with a curse."*
>
> Malachi 4:4-6

I think so many believers know in their mind that they are sons and daughters to God the Father, but they do not feel like a son on the inside. They don't feel accepted and wanted deep within. They carry unresolved conflict towards their earthly father which hinders their intimacy with the Father in heaven. They always think God is never pleased or happy with them. They never think they are good enough for Him. Why is that? What is it that is holding them back and always getting in the way of their relationship with Abba, Father? I believe it's because of the orphan heart within them. Being born again from heaven changed your identity before God the Father but didn't automatically heal the negative mindset you still have from the past. Changing the mindset and character of a human being takes time and effort. I'm definitely one of them.

An orphan heart is a heart that is fatherless in many hidden areas in our life. Maybe you're asking what an orphan heart is? Is that a biblical term? It was Jesus Himself in John 14 who uses the word orphan.

> *And I will pray the Father, and He will give you another Helper, that He may abide with you forever — the Spirit of truth, whom the world cannot receive, because it neither sees Him nor knows Him; but you know Him, for He dwells with you and will be in you. I will not leave you orphans; I will come to you.*
>
> John 14:16-18

Before we look at the attitude of the orphan heart, I want to thank Jack Frost who was the founder of Shiloh Place Ministries, and an amazing teacher on sonship. He is now sitting in the lap of Abba in heaven. Around ten years ago I went to South Carolina for one month to receive the impartation of the Father's heart and sonship. It was life-changing. I did get to meet Jack. He was a great guy who was down to earth. He was a very tall and good-looking guy. He carried the anointing of the Father's heart. Most of the material I'm writing in this chapter came from his teachings. I want to say a big thank you for what was imparted to me. Let's now look at the orphan heart.

The orphan heart is ungodly beliefs and attitudes that we have developed over a lifetime. It is manifested in our thought life, our speech, our eyes, and our attitude within us. The orphan heart is not something you can cast out. It must find its healing and identity in the heart of the Father. We will never be free from the orphan heart until we are exposed that we have one. Just because we call God our heavenly Father doesn't take away the orphan heart inside us. Why do we always struggle to feel accepted and embraced by the Father?

Why do we struggle with anger and bitterness? Why do we think God is not actively involved in our daily affairs? It's because we still have an orphan heart. Remember, an orphan heart is ungodly beliefs and attitudes that have been developed over a lifetime.

The Attitude of the Orphan Heart

- You always feel like you're on the outside looking in.
- Hard to receive correction and not very teachable.
- No tolerance for other points of view because you're always right.
- You must do something to feel good about yourself.
- You strive for the appraisal of man.
- You lead others with a need to be needed.
- You cannot forgive and harbor bitterness. You demand justice.
- You don't think people are for you and no one really cares about you.
- You're angry you never received love from your parents.
- You see leaders as a threat and source of pain.
- You always think you deserve better and always complain.
- You only value what others can do for you.
- You always have an old tape running in your mind about your past.
- You can't forgive yourself and move on.
- You don't feel comfortable with yourself. You don't respect yourself and have low self-esteem.
- You constantly judge others and lack understanding.

- You take correction as rejection.
- You don't think about the needs of others.
- You are easily offended and bothered.
- You can't be vulnerable and transparent around others.
- You always blame others for your problems.
- You don't feel like you have a special place in the Father's heart.

Wow! If I am honest with myself, I clearly see an orphan heart in many different areas in me. This list wasn't made to make you feel depressed or hopeless but was made to expose the orphan heart in all of us. This is where we begin to pursue healing and restoration. It's the doorway to the embrace of sonship.

The Embrace of Sonship

The only thing that can heal the orphan heart is the spirit of sonship. It's a journey into the Father's heart, living as a son to Abba, Father. The Father of glory wants to displace the orphan heart with a heart of sonship. It will usher us into the greatest rest we have ever experienced. Let's look again at one of the greatest chapters in scripture about sonship in Romans 8.

> *For as many as are led by the Spirit of God, these are sons of God. For you did not receive the spirit of bondage again to fear, but you received the Spirit of adoption by whom we cry out, "Abba, Father." The Spirit Himself bears witness with our spirit that we are children of God, and if children, then heirs—heirs of God and joint heirs with Christ, if indeed we suffer with Him, that we may also be glorified together.*
>
> Romans 8:14-17

The word "Abba" is an Aramaic word that corresponds to our "Daddy" or "Papa." He is the perfect Father that we never had. We have received the Spirit of adoption as sons. To be adopted means we belong to someone. We have a home, a place of acceptance, belonging, warmth, security, and affirmation. Our identity is rooted in sonship. We are heirs of God and joint heirs with Christ. We will govern nations with the Bridegroom King in the age to come. I think this is a good time to say Amen!

One of the other key chapters which reveal our sonship is found in Galatians 4. It is the companion chapter of Romans 8.

> *But when the fullness of the time had come, God sent forth His Son, born of a woman, born under the law, to redeem those who were under the law, that we might receive the adoption as sons. And because you are sons, God has sent forth the Spirit of His Son into your hearts, crying out, "Abba, Father!" <u>Therefore, you are no longer a slave but a son</u>, and if a son, then an heir of God through Christ.*
>
> Galatians 4:4-7

It is the Spirit of God's Son that makes us feel dearly loved and special. He proves to us on the inside that we belong and are fully embraced by Abba, Father. He shouts it in your spirit. One of the primary roles of the Father sending the Spirit of His Son into our hearts is for Him to cry out, Abba, Father. It is His cry being developed in us. A new paradigm is about to explode across the earth of the embrace of sonship. The Father will take His children from the mindset of a slave to the heart of a son. That's' powerful!

Let's look at the contrast between a slave and a son that we just read in Galatians 4. It is one of the core realities between the orphan heart and the heart of sonship.

Slaves: They have a master paradigm of God. They focus mostly on their work and struggle with personal relationships. They see God as a hard-taskmaster and difficult to please. Serving is a duty and not a delight. They live in fear and are motivated by mandatory obedience. They have a hard time receiving love. They never feel like they have a permanent home.

Sons: They have a Husband paradigm. They focus mostly on relationships. They see serving as a joy and a delight. They live in love and not fear. They are motivated by voluntary obedience. They see the Father as easy to please. They sense a bright smile beaming upon them from the throne of God. They feel like they always have a permanent home. Heaven is their home, and the heavenly Father is their Husband.

> *"And it shall be, in that day," Says the LORD, "That you will call Me 'My Husband,' And no longer call Me 'My Master.'*
>
> Hosea 2:16

Living as a son and not a slave is a beautiful work of God the Father in our lives. Do you realize that it takes great humility to feel beloved so profoundly as a son, because you see how bankrupt you are without having the life and presence of God's Spirit indwelling you? A son knows how needy they are before the glory of heaven. A slave thinks they can work things out on their own. They struggle to be humble.

Embracing sonship is all about receiving the outrageous love from God the Father in our spiritual journey. Unconditional love is never measured by the one receiving it, but by the One giving it. When you are convinced and receive God's unconditional acceptance and embrace, you can start loving yourself. When you love yourself, then you can start loving others. That is the progress to sonship and a life of freedom. We receive love in 1 John 3, and we give that love away in 1 John 4.

Behold what manner of love the Father has bestowed on us, that we should be called children of God! Therefore the world does not know us, because it did not know Him. Beloved, now we are children of God; and it has not yet been revealed what we shall be, but we know that when He is revealed, we shall be like Him, for we shall see Him as He is. And everyone who has this hope in Him purifies himself, just as He is pure.

1 John 3:1-3

Beloved, let us love one another, for love is of God; and everyone who loves is born of God and knows God. He who does not love does not know God, for God is love. In this the love of God was manifested toward us, that God has sent His only begotten Son into the world, that we might live through Him. In this is love, not that we loved God, but that He loved us and sent His Son to be the propitiation for our sins. Beloved, if God so loved us, we also ought to love one another. No one has seen God at any time. If we love one another, God abides in us, and His love has been perfected in us.

1 John 4:7-12

A person who knows God is a person who is at home in love. They thrive because they know they were not created for rejection, but for unconditional love and acceptance. When supernatural love from heaven is poured out in the earth, that is when revival will break out, and signs and wonders will follow. Revival begins at home when a family is transformed by the Father's passionate love, and other families want it. Revival begins when marriages and children are transformed through the embrace of sonship, and they become God's voice to the broken hearted. Revival begins with my family and me.

Beloved, do you realize that the Father who reigns supremely in heaven loves us the same way He loves His own precious Son? This speaks volumes! How much does the Father burn with passion for Jesus His Son? Meditate upon that reality!

> *I in them, and You in Me; that they may be made perfect in one, and that the world may know that You have sent Me, and have loved them as You have loved Me.*
>
> John 17:23

I remember when I was having lunch with Pastor Greg of Antioch Community Church in Knoxville, Tennessee. The worship is just like IHOPKC, and the teaching is very good. He was sharing about the outrageous love of God and used a perfect illustration of a train which reflects who He is. He said; "when a train goes by you can hear and feel the rumbling of it. It's unstoppable and immovable. Jesus' love is like this. You can sense the rumblings of His presence. The force behind cannot be stopped. **He's cranking the horn, saying; "I LOVE YOU."** Next time you hear the horn coming from a train, remember what your God is saying to you."

8 Distinct Titles of God the Father

1. He is the Father of the Lord Jesus Christ (see Ephesians 1:3).
2. He is the Father of glory (see Ephesians 1:17).
3. He is the Father of compassion (see 2 Corinthians 1:3).
4. He is Abba, Father (see Romans 8:15).
5. He is the Father of Lights (see James 1:17).
6. He is our Father in heaven (see Matthew 6:9).
7. He is the Father of the fatherless (see Psalm 68:5).
8. He is the Everlasting Father (see Isaiah 9:6).

Being Sons of the Most High

I want to conclude with one of the most challenging passages in scripture of the reality and what it looks like to embrace the life of sonship. This passage is found in Luke 6 and is from the heart of Jesus to His followers. After Jesus lays out how we are to live on the earth by forgiving our enemies, He ends with a reward by saying; *You will be sons of the Most High.*

> *But if you love those who love you, what credit is that to you? For even sinners love those who love them. And if you do good to those who do good to you, what credit is that to you? For even sinners do the same. And if you lend to those from whom you hope to receive back, what credit is that to you? For even sinners lend to sinners to receive as much back. But love your enemies, do good, and lend, hoping for nothing in return; and your reward will be great, and <u>you will be sons of the Most High.</u> For He is kind to the unthankful and evil. Therefore be merciful, just as your Father also is merciful.*
>
> Luke 6:27-36

This portion of scripture is not talking about salvation because how can we forgive if we don't have the indwelling Spirit. The day we got born again we became sons of the Most High. There are no conditions to salvation. It is by grace through faith we are saved. I believe what Jesus is saying is how we will be rewarded when we love our enemies, do good, lend, be kind to the unthankful and evil person, and be merciful. Then we reap the reward of feeling like a son on the inside. When we put into practice what Jesus is saying, our reward will be great. We will start feeling fully cherished, accepted, wanted, and beloved in the Father's heart. That's the reward! We are sons through the finished work of the cross, but we start experiencing a whole different level and anointing of sonship when we forgive our enemies.

Sonship releases your inheritance!

Justice is good, but mercy is better. If you spend eighty percent of the time demanding justice, then the enemy has the right to beat you eighty percent of the time. You must surrender your judgments towards those who have hurt you and choose to forgive. Most judgments are rooted in hurt and bitterness. The hurt is usually connected to a lack of total love and acceptance. Now is the time to receive the supernatural breaking forth of the fire and power of the Fathers amazing love in the deepest areas of your wounds. He is willing to pour it out upon you, but are you willing to receive it, and hold on to it?

Beloved, I encourage you to go deep into what Jesus profoundly shared in Luke 6. You will experience the embrace of sonship like never before. You will become a voice to the voiceless. It will usher you into your inheritance. You will lead others into a divine encounter with Abba, Father. Amen!

I have a chart that Jack Frost put together of the contrast between the orphan heart and sonship. It is brilliant. You can place it on the refrigerator for your remembrance. You can take it to your bible study and go over it together as a group. I believe you will enter the embrace of sonship. You are sons of the Most High!

Orphan Heart Vs. the Heart of Sonship

See God as Master	IMAGE OF GOD	See God as loving Father
Independent / Self-reliant	DEPENDENCY	Independence / Acknowledges Need
Live by the Love of Law	THEOLOGY	Live by the Law of Love
Insecure / Lack peace	SECURITY	Rest and Peace
Strive for the Praise, approval, and acceptance of man	NEED FOR APPROVAL	Totally accepted in God's love and justified by grace
A need for personal achievement as you seek to impress God and others, or no motivation to serve all	MOTIVE FOR SERVICE	Service that is motivated by a deep gratitude for being unconditionally loved and accepted by God
Duty and earning God's favor or no motivations at all	MOTIVE BEHIND CHRISTIAN DISCIPLINES	Pleasure and delight
"Must" be holy to have God's favor, thus increasing a sense of shame and guilt	MOTIVE FOR PURITY	"Want to" be holy; do not want anything to hinder an intimate relationship with God
Self-rejection from comparing yourself to others	SELF-IMAGE	Positive and affirmed because you know you have such value to God
Seek comfort in counterfeit affections: addictions, compulsions, escapism, busyness, hyper-religious activity	SOURCE OF COMFORT	Seek times of quietness and solitude to rest in the Father's presence and love

Competition, rivalry, and jealousy toward others' success and position	PEER RELATIONSHIPS	Humility and unity as you value others and are able to rejoice in their blessings and success
Accusation and exposure in order to make yourself look good by making others look bad	HANDLING OTHERS' FAULTS	Love covers as you seek to restore others in a spirit of love and gentleness
See authority as a source of pain; distrustful toward them and lack a heart attitude of submission	VIEW OF AUTHORITY	Respectful, honoring; you see them as ministers of God for good in your life
Difficulty receiving admonition; you must be right, so you easily get your feelings hurt and close your spirit to discipline	VIEW OF ADMONITION	See the receiving of admonition as a blessing and need in your life so that your faults and weaknesses are exposed and put to death
Guarded and conditional; based upon others' performance as you seek to get your own needs met	EXPRESSION OF LOVE	Open, patient, and affectionate as you lay your life and agendas down in order to meet the needs of others
Conditional & Distant	SENSE OF GOD'S PRESENCE	Close & Intimate
Bondage	CONDITION	Liberty
Feel like a Servant / Slave	POSITION	Feel like a Son/Daughter
Spiritual ambition; the earnest desire for some spiritual achievement and distinction and the willingness to strive for it; a desire to be seen and counted among the mature.	VISION	To daily experience the Father's unconditional love and acceptance and then be sent as a representative of His love to family and others.
Fight for what you can get!	FUTURE	Sonship releases your inheritance!

CHAPTER 6
The Throne of God

If there was one chapter in scripture that focuses specifically on the throne of God, it would be Revelation 4. It is the crescendo of the beauty realm of God. This is what our present generation needs so desperately. Having more ministry activities and church programs is good, but having a fresh revelation of the beauty realm of heaven is most powerful. It produces wonder, fascination and, marvel. It will usher us into our destiny!

The Glory of Revelation 4

John the Apostle sees a vision of majesty and splendor surrounding the throne of God. He is invited into an open door (portal) in heaven and sees God the Father portrayed in terms of brilliant shining diamonds. He describes the throne room of heaven in the holy of holies. He sees a sea of glass like crystal across the throne room with incredible flashes of swirling light shimmering from the throne, and lightning's everywhere. Ezekiel the prophet describes the sea of glass as sparkling like ice and awesome (see Ezekiel 1:22). John hears loud and terrifying peals and rumblings of thunder which causes him to tremble. The God of glory thunders. He hears the most glorious song that is sung day and night by the seraphim; *Holy, holy, holy, Lord God Almighty, Who was and is and is to come!* The Seraphim are the highest order of the angelic hosts. They are called "the burning ones." When the twenty-four elders hear this anointed song like a choir in perfect harmony, they cast their crowns before the throne, saying; *You are Worthy O Lord.* He beholds seven huge torches of fire burning before the throne with an emerald rainbow encircling the throne. What beauty!

When you first read this chapter, it will feel kinda awkward because it's heavenly language, and no man has ever seen God the Father. You will struggle at first with the words, but if you stick with it and press into God, you will get a heavenly breakthrough. This is where the God whom you love and worship abides. It's where you will be in your future because it's your inheritance. And by faith, you can now tap into the beauty realm because your citizenship is in heaven. You don't have to wait until you get to heaven to experience the supernatural realm of heaven. Let's go ahead and delve into this glorious chapter.

> *After these things I looked, and behold, a door standing open in heaven. And the first voice which I heard was like a trumpet speaking with me, saying, "Come up here, and I will show you things which must take place after this." Immediately I was in the Spirit; and behold, a throne set in heaven, and One sat on the throne. And He who sat there was like a jasper and a sardius stone in appearance; and there was a rainbow around the throne, in appearance like an emerald. Around the throne were twenty-four thrones, and on the thrones I saw twenty-four elders sitting, clothed in white robes; and they had crowns of gold on their heads. And from the throne proceeded lightnings, thunderings, and voices. Seven lamps of fire were burning before the throne, which are the seven Spirits of God. Before the throne there was a sea of glass, like crystal. And in the midst of the throne, and*

around the throne, were four living creatures full of eyes in front and in back. The first living creature was like a lion, the second living creature like a calf, the third living creature had a face like a man, and the fourth living creature was like a flying eagle. The four living creatures, each having six wings, were full of eyes around and within. And they do not rest day or night, saying: "Holy, holy, holy, Lord God Almighty, Who was and is and is to come!" Whenever the living creatures give glory and honor and thanks to Him who sits on the throne, who lives forever and ever, the twenty-four elders fall down before Him who sits on the throne and worship Him who lives forever and ever, and cast their crowns before the throne, saying: "You are worthy, O Lord, To receive glory and honor and power; For You created all things, And by Your will they exist and were created."

Revelation 4:1-11

The word "behold" in Revelation 4:1 is not a whisper, but is shouted throughout the universe. It means to stand in amazement or to wonder. It's a call to gaze, a call to attention. It is used to signal our attention. Something very dramatic and very definitive is being communicated. The power behind the throne is the power of beholding. The very first thing John saw was the throne of God. What a sight it must have been for him. When we talk about the throne of God we are talking about God's Kingdom, government and His Sovereignty over the entire earth.

There is a throne which guarantees that God's plans will come to pass. The throne is not empty, but One is sitting upon it and is planning, acting, intervening and praying for us. A real person is at the government center of the universe, and none can challenge Him. He is in full control over everything that's going on in our lives. Hallelujah!

Embracing the Sovereignty of God

I will give you the most simple and accurate definition of what sovereignty means: God is God, and we are not. Pretty profound! It's not that difficult to understand but is a challenge to practically live out. He is infinite, and we are finite. He is all knowing and we are limited. God the Father is the supreme ruler of every human being. He calls the shots from above and orchestrates His plans and purposes on the earth. We know by knowledge that there is a God in heaven, but we must have a fresh awareness of a living God sitting upon the throne. It will change the way we live our lives. It will cause us to embrace the sovereignty of God.

The sovereignty of God is like a great mystery. We must learn to live in the realm of mystery and embrace it. It's what brings us into a faith that attracts the invasion of God. Many times we don't fully understand what He is doing in our lives. We struggle when we can't seem to figure Him out, but that is normal because the scriptures say that God's ways and thoughts are higher than ours.

> *For My thoughts are not your thoughts, Nor are your ways My ways, says the LORD. For as the heavens are higher than the earth, So are My ways higher than your ways, And My thoughts than your thoughts.*
>
> Isaiah 55:8-9

If we don't fully embrace the sovereignty of God in our daily lives, we will become easily offended by His leadership. Offense goes against the core of God's heart because He is always good (see Psalm 136). We looked at offense earlier in chapter three. It's an important word to search out. The word "offense" means a stumbling block. People in ancient days would take a block of wood and put it in front of someone who was blind, and as they fell they would laugh. That's where we get the word offense. It was Jesus Himself who pronounced a blessing to those who are not offended at Him.

And blessed is he who is not offended because of Me.

Matthew 11:6

There are different reasons why we as the bride of Christ get offended at God, but I believe one of the main reasons is because of our demands we put upon Him. We might not think we do or even speak out loud about demanding from Him, but it's tucked away in our thought life. When we don't get our way with God, we start building a case against Him. I like what Bill Johnson says: "people who insist on having a legal contract with God will end up broken. The reason is that we become rigid in demanding from God and that place of arrogance must be broken. God is more passionate about our intimacy with Him than our comfort. As we become thankful for what we have we remove all weapons from the enemies' hands."

All of our suffering and trials are either initiated or allowed by God Himself. The reason you are going through so much difficulty is not that there is something wrong with you or God is mad at you. He is preparing you for the greatest day of your life. It's the day you partner closely with Him during the millennial reign on the earth. We cannot recognize God's wisdom unless we know the end towards which He is working. He knows something we don't. He sees something we don't. He sees the big picture from high above. He believes in us as no one else does, and that's why we need to trust His sovereignty. We need to surrender our demands because God doesn't owe us anything. We owe Him. He brought us out of the eternal darkness and invited us into a love relationship with Him. He knows exactly what He is doing. His understanding governing our lives upon the throne is unsearchable. This is the beauty of the One upon the throne of God.

> *"To whom then will you liken Me, Or to whom shall I be equal?" says the Holy One. Lift up your eyes on high, And see who has created these things, Who brings out their host by number; He calls them all by name, By the greatness of His might And the strength of His power; Not one is missing. Why do you say, O Jacob, And speak, O Israel: "My way is hidden from the LORD, And my just claim is passed over by my God?" Have you not known? Have you not heard? The everlasting God, the LORD, The Creator of the ends of the earth, Neither faints nor is weary. His understanding is unsearchable.*
>
> Isaiah 40:25-28

Understanding God's Leadership upon the Throne

God the Father has a vision for each and every believer. His will in our lives cannot be stopped. There is nothing which happens by accident. His plan is perfect with a bright hope of a future (see Jeremiah 29:11). **He has a crazy and wild story for you**. So what is the Father's eternal and grand plan upon the throne? It's to have an equally yoked mature bride made ready for His Beloved Son, at the marriage of the Lamb.

> *Let us be glad and rejoice and give Him glory, for the marriage of the Lamb has come, and His wife has made herself ready.*
>
> Revelation 19:7

Once we understand this glorious plan from heaven's throne, we can then better interpret the daily circumstances in our lives, and submit to His divine leadership over us. The heavenly Father has great passion and zeal to make sure the bride will be ready for the wedding day. That's why He's called the sardius God in Revelation 4.

> *And He who sat there was like a jasper and a sardius stone in appearance; and there was a rainbow around the throne, in appearance like an emerald.*
>
> Revelation 4:3

The sardius stone is a deep red diamond which reveals the Father's burning passion and desire for us. He has deep feelings for His sons and daughters. It's His relentless fiery love to want us more than anyone can imagine. Maybe sometimes you think that nobody wants you. You feel unwanted. But the sardius God upon the throne wants you. He accepts you wholeheartedly.

> *To the praise of the glory of His grace, by which <u>He made us accepted in the Beloved</u>.*
>
> Ephesians 1:6

The Bible says that God is love in 1 John 4. But to put it more profoundly, **God is a lover**! That is who He is forever. It is why He chose to fight for you because He is a sardius God. The writer of Hebrews calls Him a jealous God, an all-consuming fire. Because of His zeal for you to come close to Him, He will remove everything that hinders love. His discipline and conviction of sin is not His anger directed at you, but it's His love and mercy to get everything out of the way, so He can fully possess you. That's the emerald stone in Revelation 4:3 which portrays the mercy of God with a brilliant rainbow encircling the throne. He desires to be close and intimate with you. He will fight for you and never let you go. **His leadership over your life is perfect**. Don't let the enemy tell you that you're not on the right path, and you are not in the center of God's will. Because you know God's heart is steadfast and He never changes, you can submit to His divine leadership. He will never mislead you or forsake you.

> *For He Himself has said, "I will never leave you nor forsake you." So we may boldly say: "The LORD is my helper; I will not fear. What can man do to me?"*
>
> Hebrews 13:5-6

A Man upon the Throne of God

Ezekiel the prophet had an incredible revelation of Jesus as a Man upon the throne of God. He is pictured ruling and reigning high above on the throne. Perhaps the prophet wondered how a human could be exalted so high at the very top of God's government. Let's look at Ezekiel 1 and get caught up in the throne room.

> *And above the firmament (sea of glass) over their heads was the likeness of a throne, in appearance like a sapphire stone; on the likeness of the throne was a likeness with the appearance of a man high above it. Also from the appearance of His waist and upward I saw, as it were, the color of amber (glowing metal) with the appearance of fire all around within it; and from the appearance of His waist and downward I saw, as it were, the appearance of fire with brightness all around. Like the appearance of a rainbow in a cloud on a rainy day, so was the appearance of the brightness all around it. This was the appearance of the likeness of the glory of the LORD.*
>
> Ezekiel 1:26-28

Jesus, the God-Man, is pictured sitting upon a sapphire (deep blue) throne above the sea of glass with the four living creatures below the expanse. He is described as glowing metal, full of fire from His waist up and His waist down. He is consumed with divine fire, and a brilliant light radiates and surrounds His entire being. I call Jesus the Man of fire!

The government will rest completely upon Jesus' shoulders (see Isaiah 9:6). He alone will bear the burden. There will be an ongoing increase of His kingdom coming to the earth. Let it be trumpeted loud and clear: heaven is coming to the earth. The Man upon the throne is coming to transform the entire globe for the glory and passion of His Father. He will prepare the earth as the place for God the Father to usher in His glorious palace (see Revelation 21).

Can you believe it? The government of God's kingdom will rest completely upon the shoulders of the Man Christ Jesus. A Man will rule the entire earth and take full responsibility to carry the load. He must stoop in order to lift; He must almost disappear under the load before He incredibly straightens His back, and marches with the whole mass swaying on His shoulders. What strength, what wisdom, what might, and what determination. We must keep this truth in mind: The One who bore the sins of the earth at Calvary is going to bear the weight of the entire earth upon His shoulders as a human when He returns to the earth. I don't know which is more amazing; the transcendent God becoming human, or a Man sitting above the circle of the earth reigning on His throne.

Beloved, this is a good time to fix your gaze upon the glory of God's throne. The One who is sitting at the vast top of God's empire is not passive, and He doesn't want you to be passive. He wants you to pursue Him; to reach and stretch for what you have never obtained before. He wants you to trust Him completely. He desires that you allow Him to direct and orchestrate the very details of your life and family. That's what He does best. There is one thing you can fully count on: Jesus is an amazing and perfect leader!

The One Upon the Throne is Holy, Yet Intimate

The scriptures over and over declare that God the Father is holy. He is transcendent. He dwells in a high and holy place and is separated from everything that is common.

> *For thus says the High and Lofty One Who inhabits eternity, whose name is Holy: I dwell in the high and holy place, With him who has a contrite and humble spirit, To revive the spirit of the humble, And to revive the heart of the contrite ones.*
>
> Isaiah 57:15

This passage is the great paradox of God's heart. The One upon the throne is holy, yet intimate. He dwells in a high and holy place fully separated from the stain of sin and darkness, but abides and lives with the humble. He hangs out with the small guys like you and I. He draws near to those who need Him and want Him. He desires an intimate relationship with the humble. Most kings on the earth focus on their power and not love. This King of glory is different – He is more focused on burning love and desire. He not only wants to love upon us as no one else can, but He wants to entrust us with authority and power. He is passionate and excited to share His leadership with us. He wants to enthrone and crown us as kings and priests before the glory of heaven. He's not threatened or intimidated to share His power like other kings are. It is why we see the twenty-four elders wearing crowns of gold and casting them before the throne of God in Revelation 4.

> *The twenty-four elders fall down before Him who sits on the throne and worship Him who lives forever and ever, and cast their crowns before the throne, saying: "You are worthy, O Lord, To receive glory and honor and power; For You created all things, And by Your will they exist and were created."*
>
> Revelation 4:10-11

The sardius King upon the throne is very intimate and desires a personal love relationship with Him. He doesn't want your religion for He hates it. He wants you. He is not an emotionless God, and He's not a distant God which many portray Him to be. He is very near and closer to you than you think. How can He turn His back on you when He has inscribed you on the palms of His hands?

> *But Zion said, "The L*ORD *has forsaken me, And my Lord has forgotten me." Can a woman forget her nursing child, And not have compassion on the son of her womb? Surely they may forget, Yet I will not forget you. See, I have inscribed you on the palms of My hands; Your walls are continually before Me.*
>
> Isaiah 49:14-16

Beloved, because you are God's prized possession, He wants to revive you and make your heart come alive again. He wants passion for Jesus to be the banner over your life. He wants to partner with you in your divine calling, but it will take a contrite spirit to get His full attention. God opposes the proud. He loves those who stoop low at His Sons' feet in utter dependence. It's time to go low. It's time to bend our knee because the sardius God upon the throne is very interested in you. He is interested in your family and marriage. He's interested in your kiddos. He is interested in your business and your ministry. Let Him revive you with His unyielding passion like never before, so you can have intimacy with the One who dwells in a high and holy place.

You will never be disappointed or let down by the flame of love that's in the heart of the beautiful God on His throne. Maybe you heard a thousand times that God loves you which He does. But to make it more personal, **He really likes you**. You're not a burden to Him. His sardius passion will sustain you in the darkest times. His passion for you will carry you and strengthen you in the midst of the wilderness. Here is the absolute truth about One sitting upon the throne - He will always love you one hundred percent. Forever!

> *The LORD has appeared of old to me, saying: Yes, I have loved you with an everlasting love; Therefore with loving kindness I have drawn you.*
>
> Jeremiah 31:3

The Father's Throne is a Fiery Flame

What a stunning sight! Daniel the prophet sees a river of fire flowing from the throne of God. A hundred million of angels are worshiping and adoring the fiery flame of God the Father (Ancient of Days). Let's enter into the divine drama of heaven in this heart moving passage.

> *I kept looking Until thrones were set up, And the Ancient of Days took His seat; His vesture (garment) was like white snow And the hair of His head like pure wool. His throne was ablaze with flames, Its wheels were a burning fire. "<u>A river of fire was flowing And coming out from before Him</u>; Thousands upon thousands were attending Him, And myriads upon myriads were standing before Him; The court sat, And the books were opened.*
>
> Daniel 7:9-10 (NASB)

The atmosphere of the throne room of heaven is energized and blazing with the fire of God's glory. It's the fire of holy romance. This river of fire flowing from the throne is a picture of the Holy Spirit imparting divine passion to our hearts. Remember, passion for Jesus comes from discovering His passion for us. The river of fire is the activity of the Holy Spirit, ebbing and flowing before the throne. It is a raging stream coming from the being of God Himself. He wants to impart this raging fire inside us. The Ancient of Days is seated upon His fiery throne, and His garment is white as snow. Imagine with me the dramatic colors of white and red. We are talking about the brightest red and the purest white combined together. It is the passion and purity of God Himself. This is why there are ten thousand times ten thousand angels ministering before Him. The Father who sits upon a blazing throne is the center of attention. May we be found and caught up right in the middle of it all.

This holy fire that proceeds from the throne is our destiny. It is beauty and romance at its highest. It is the place we are to abide and camp out. I just love to picture the river of fire streaming over me as I stand upon the crystal sea of glass. It sets my heart aflame. In Revelation 15:2, the sea of glass is mingled with flaming fire. I believe the river of fire flowing from God's throne is being poured out onto the sea of glass, which sets ablaze those who are standing and dancing upon it. **Forever we will dance upon the sea of glass with our Beloved**. It's a perfect reflection of dazzling beauty. As we stand on the sea of glass by faith, we are putting ourselves right in the middle of a raging torrent. It is the place to be utterly consumed by God Himself.

> *And I saw something like a sea of glass mingled with fire, and those who have the victory over the beast, over his image and over his mark and over the number of his name, standing on the sea of glass, having harps of God. They sing the song of Moses, the servant of God, and the song of the Lamb, saying: Great and marvelous are Your works, Lord God Almighty! Just and true are Your ways, O King of the saints!*
>
> Revelation 15:2-3

The Jasper God

As we come to the end of this chapter on the throne of God, I want to look at the glorious splendor of the jasper God in Revelation 4. I don't know about you, but I just love the jasper God.

> *And He who sat there was like a jasper and a sardius stone in appearance; and there was a rainbow around the throne, in appearance like an emerald.*
> Revelation 4:3

John saw God the Father revealed in three distinct diamonds (jasper, sardius, emerald) through an open-door visitation. The jasper stone is a radiant white diamond of clearest luster. It's clear as crystal and shines forth the light and splendor of the Father's glory. The jasper stone reveals what God looks like.

In Job 37, Asaph describes God as full of awesome majesty. If you want your heart to be fascinated, then the majesty realm is right down your path.

> *He comes from the north as golden splendor; <u>With God is awesome majesty</u>. As for the Almighty, we cannot find Him; He is excellent in power, In judgment and abundant justice; He does not oppress.*
> Job 37:22-23

Robert H. Mounce, the author of The Book of Revelation, writes, "…God is portrayed as the brilliance of light reflected from precious stones…" His glory is like the radiance of a brilliant white diamond. This is the revelation John received about the indescribable jasper God.

In Isaiah 6, we have a picture of God's jasper glory and holiness that will fill the whole earth. The seraphim cover their eyes at His penetrating splendor. They are awestruck at the blinding presence of the King. This is the place and atmosphere where we bow in the brilliance of His beauty. Just like Isaiah, may we have the same testimony: *For my eyes have seen the King, the Lord of Hosts.* Just like the Seraphim, may we proclaim and sing; *Holy, holy, holy is the Lord of Hosts; the whole earth is full of His glory.*

> *In the year that King Uzziah died, I saw the Lord sitting on a throne, high and lifted up, and the train of His robe filled the temple. Above it stood seraphim; each one had six wings: with two he covered his face, with two he covered his feet, and with two he flew. And one cried to another and said: "Holy, holy, holy is the LORD of hosts; The whole earth is full of His glory!" And the posts of the door were shaken by the voice of him who cried out, and the house was filled with smoke. So I said: "Woe is me, for I am undone! Because I am a man of unclean lips, And I dwell in the midst of a people of unclean lips; For my eyes have seen the King, The LORD of hosts."*
>
> Isaiah 6:1-5

Beloved, the jasper God is so beautiful and majestic and dwells in unapproachable light. He is called the "Father of Lights." He is shining in absolute beauty high upon His throne, and the earth is overflowing with His glory. His beaming light is transcendent, immeasurably above the entire created universe. Breath-taking splendor flows from God's jasper being. All that surrounds Him is divine entertainment at its highest. It is the Father's jasper glory which the bride so desperately needs. May we be radically undone before His throne, as we set our gaze upon His jasper glory. May we be fascinated with the majesty of the throne room of God. May we contend and pursue an open heaven (portal) visitation of the beauty realm of God. What John saw through the open door in heaven is the glory of the jasper God that will cover the earth.

> *For the earth will be filled with the knowledge of the glory of the LORD, As the waters cover the sea.*
>
> Habakkuk 2:14

CHAPTER 7
The Beauty of God

The study and pursuit of the beauty of God has been my life vision. The Lord made it clear in 1999 when I joined the International House of Prayer of Kansas City that it would be my main focus for my life. The passage that God gave me was the one that conquered king David's heart and transformed him into a man after God's own heart. It was the secret to his journey in God!

> *One thing I have desired of the LORD, That will I seek: That I may dwell in the house of the LORD All the days of my life, To behold the beauty of the LORD, And to inquire in His temple.*
>
> Psalm 27:4

Being a Person of One Thing

The power of this verse and the principle of David's life lies in the words "one thing." Now David wasn't exaggerating when he wrote this. This was real and personal to him. I believe we have many desires in our personal life. It's why we have so many distractions because we want way too many things. There is nothing wrong with wanting other things, but what's the most important desire we have? David didn't say that one thing was his only desire, but was saying "to behold the beauty of the Lord" was the premier thing that gripped and occupied his life.

The one thing we should desire most is to gaze upon the beauty of God all the days of our lives. We cannot do this on the run. It takes time and perseverance to get alone with God and receive a fresh revelation of His beauty and splendor. David contended for this lifestyle. Being a king wasn't his dream, but spending all His days gazing upon God's beauty was his dream. It was his compelling pursuit. He pressed into God because he knew that any other desire would fade away compared to the endless beauty of God's heart.

We will be challenged into the radicalness of what this verse is talking about. It will be disruptive. We might even lose friends along the way. But what's important to you? What do you desire most in life? What is it you want to offer the beautiful God when you see Him face to face? Only you will be able to answer and respond to this "one thing" pursuit. There are no shortcuts. No one can do it for you. You are the one who needs to go after and fight for the preciousness of it.

> *Fight the good fight of faith, lay hold on eternal life, to which you were also called and have confessed the good confession in the presence of many witnesses.*
>
> 1 Timothy 6:12

Keeping First Things First

I believe the Lord would whisper from heaven that if we keep first things first in our lives, He will give us other things in His timing. **It's time we lose ourselves in beholding the beauty of God and His kingdom**. I remember in 2001 as I was seeking the Lord and reading Psalm 27:4, I clearly heard the Lord speak to me by asking me a question. He said, what is it you want most in life? It's like He gave me a blank check to fill in whatever I wanted. Now I'm not trying to be haughty, but without hesitation, I said with all my being as tears flowed down my face that I wanted to gaze upon His beauty all the days of my life. I wanted to keep first things first. This is what I wanted most in life. After I answered God's question, I sensed His presence and delight in a powerful way. It was precious!

Let me share something that might relate to some of you. By the grace of God, I know what it's like to be fully locked into gazing upon God's beauty. I know what it's like to have my heart fully alive and empowered. But I also know what it's like to get off track of the one thing pursuit, as my heart was definitely not alive. I would call it drifting away from my first love. But the good news for us is that we have not gone too far from the magnet of God's love. There is hope; you can get back that sense of His nearness if you want it. You can jump into the river of God's beauty right now. You can get back on track to keep first things first because you are a lover of God!

Determined to Search Out God's Beauty

The beauty of God is what our present generation needs most. We must be intentional in searching it out. It is a vast subject that we will never outgrow. It's endless beauty to discover. A billion years from now we will see and learn new things about Jesus that will fascinate our heart. It is the divine treasure hunt to pursue. Are you ready for a radical change in your life? Do you want to go on a treasure hunt that will consume you, seeking out different aspects of God's radiant beauty? There will be the suddenly of God surprise when you least expect it. Will you fully embrace the "one thing" pursuit? Will you be determined to aggressively search out God's beauty like never before?

Beloved, I'm making this radical commitment to the "one thing" pursuit even as I'm writing my book. Let's go together and stay determined not to allow anything to get us off track. If you are sincerely ready to make this commitment, I will leave my email at the back of my book, and feel free to reach out and share your testimony or struggle with the "one thing" pursuit. I will definitely get back with you. I would like to grow a team on this radical subject.

Before you continue reading, I think it's a good time that I say a prayer for you. Let's pray: Lord Jesus, I thank you for my beloved friends who are at a place in their lives where they must have more. Would You come and awaken their heart and unveil the beauty of who You are and what You will do for them. Satisfy the cry and longing within them. Let them discover and feel your holy passion for them. Take them on an adventure into the treasure of Your hidden beauty, in Jesus' name. Amen!

What do you think is the greatest benefit and reward when we discover and encounter the beauty of God? I believe the greatest reward of discovering God's beauty is a lovesick heart. The word lovesick is mentioned two times in the Song of Solomon.

> *Sustain me with cakes of raisins, Refresh me with apples, For I am lovesick.*
>
> Song of Solomon 2:5

> *I charge you, O daughters of Jerusalem, If you find my beloved, That you tell him I am lovesick!*
>
> Song of Solomon 5:8

A lovesick person for Jesus is very powerful on the inside. They cannot be controlled or manipulated by man. You cannot persuade them to do anything that would hinder the closeness of their lovesick heart to God. They really don't count the cost or believe they are paying a big price to serve Jesus because the reward of gazing upon His beauty pays so well. To see God is the fuel to lovesickness.

I want to give you five aspects or themes of the beauty of God. They are not the only ones but are the main ones. I encourage you to pursue them and go deep until you are conquered by the "one thing" pursuit. Does that sound good?

Five Aspects of God's Beauty

1. The beauty of creation (Job 38-39).

2. The beauty of the cross (Isaiah 53).

3. The beauty of the bride (Song of Solomon 6).

4. The beauty of heaven (Revelation 21-22).

5. The beauty of God Himself (Psalm 86).

The Beauty of God in the Book of Revelation

I believe the beauty of God crescendos the most in the book of Revelation. Most believers debate about dates and charts over this book. They miss the whole purpose. The first five words in chapter one say; *The revelation of Jesus Christ*. The Greek word for "revelation" is Apocalypse. It means to unveil. God, the father, is going to unveil the beauty of His Son, so all the nations will worship Him. He's going to pull back the veil and let the bride of Christ discover His beauty and glory like never before. God's beauty will be poured out across the earth through the book of Revelation. Let's peer into eight different chapters which portray the beauty of God. I call it "the beauty realm of God." It's just a simple outline for you to study and delve into.

1. The Beauty of the Son of Man (Revelation 1)

- Jesus is the ruler over the kings of the earth.
- Jesus passionately loves and forgives us.
- Jesus is coming with the clouds to the earth.
- Jesus is clothed in a beautiful garment.
- Jesus' hair is white as snow.
- Jesus' voice is like the sound of many waters.
- Jesus' face shines brighter than the sun.

2. The Beauty of God the Father (Revelation 4)
- The Father sits in supremacy on His throne.
- The Father is like a jasper diamond.
- The Father is like a sardius diamond.
- The Father is like an emerald diamond.
- Lightnings and thunderings before the throne.
- A sea of glass like pure crystal.
- The transcendent beauty of the Lord.
- Twenty-four elders cast their crowns before the throne.
- The Father is Worthy.

3. The Beauty of the Worthy Lamb of God (Revelation 5)
- Jesus takes the scroll from the Father.
- Jesus is the Lion of Judah - worthy to open the scroll.
- Jesus is the slain Lamb.
- The harp & bowl of worship & prayer.
- Worthy is the Lamb who was slain.
- The voice of thousands and thousands of angels.

4. The Beauty of the Great Multitude (Revelation 7)
- A great multitude is standing before the throne.
- All the nations are clothed in white garments.
- They have palm branches in their hands crying, salvation.
- The Lamb is their Shepherd.
- God will wipe every tear away.

5. The Beauty of the Lamb and the 144,000 Jewish believers (Revelation 14)
   - The Lamb is standing on Mount Zion.
   - The voice of many waters and loud thunder.
   - The sound of harpists playing their harps.
   - A new song before the throne.
   - They follow the Lamb wherever He goes.
   - One like a Son of Man sitting on a cloud

6. The Beauty of the Sea of Glass (Revelation 15)
   - The Sea of Glass is mingled with holy fire.
   - Great and marvelous are God's works.
   - All nations will come and worship God.
   - The temple was filled with smoke.

7. The Beauty of the marriage of the Lamb (Revelation 19)
   - A loud voice of a great multitude in heaven.
   - The voice of many waters.
   - The sound of mighty thundering's.
   - The bride dressed in clean and bright garments.
   - The Bridegroom Judge is on a white horse.
   - The Lamb's eyes are like a flame of fire.
   - There are many crowns on Jesus' head.
   - Jesus is clothed with a robe dipped in blood.
   - The armies of heaven are clothed in white linen.

- On Jesus' robe and on His thigh a name written: KING OF KINGS AND LORD OF LORDS.

8. The Beauty of the Bride and the New Jerusalem (Revelation 21-22)
- The holy city New Jerusalem is coming down out of heaven.
- A bride adorned for her Husband.
- God will wipe away every tear from their eye.
- He who overcomes shall be My son.
- The bride, the Lamb's wife.
- Her light was like a jasper stone.
- Twelve gates were twelve pearls.
- The Lamb is its Light.
- A pure river is flowing from the throne and the Lamb.
- They shall see God's face.
- Behold, I am coming quickly.
- The Root and Offspring of David.
- The Bright and Morning Star.
- The Spirit and the bride say, "Come!"

Just as we looked at eight different chapters of the beauty of God, I want to give you eight practical things that you can do to behold and encounter God's beauty. Focus upon one at a time and ask the Holy Spirit to fascinate you with God's beauty.

How Do We Behold the Beauty of God?

First: We encounter God's beauty as we feed on the scriptures of God's personality and emotions. I believe the chapters that we just glimpsed at in the Book of Revelation is a great place to start. We are to behold, meditate, sing, and proclaim the beauty of God. Let the Word of God be your best friend.

Second: We say Yes to becoming a person of "one thing." We make a holy determination to live this lifestyle and be intentional to search out the deep things of God's beauty. Like King David, we want to encounter and experience it as a holy preoccupation. Beholding God's beauty is more than delightful, it's transforming.

Third: We spend time in worship. I encourage you to purchase or download worship songs that move your heart. Honestly, there is not a day in my life where I haven't played worship music at some point during the day. It helps my heart to come alive and tenderizes my spirit to receive the Word of God.

Fourth: We cultivate a prayer life with Jesus, the Bridegroom. We speak the Word of God out loud in prayer so our faith can grow. Faith comes by hearing the Word of God. Pray for God to give you divine might in your inner man. Pray for Him to open and rend the heavens.

Fifth: We sing the Word of God out loud. This is one of my favorite things to do. You don't have to have a good voice to do it. When you sing the Word, you don't use your mind but your spirit. The Holy Spirit takes the information on the pages of scripture and downloads it inside your heart, so you can start feeling what your reading. When you feel what your reading, you have now tapped into the spirit of revelation. There is something very powerful that happens when you start singing the beauty of God in the scriptures. Play worship music in the background. Sing to God, but sing from His heart to your heart. It's more powerful. Have fun!

Sixth: We throw in some fasting. If you want to speed up and accelerate the encounter of God's beauty then fasting is something you should be doing. It tenderizes your spirit and makes your more sensitive to the Holy Spirit. It produces voluntary weakness.

Seventh: We start writing down the thoughts and inspiration that God gives us throughout the day. It's called journaling. You don't need to be an author to do this. When you write down on paper what God is showing you, the revelation starts to grow. It becomes more clear to you.

Eighth: We gaze upon God's beauty by being still. **Stillness removes clutter**. Our minds are easily distracted and roam around all over the place. We have to train our mind to be focused. At first, it will be very difficult as you will realize how much your mind wanders. Have a scripture that focuses on God's beauty and start dwelling and meditating upon it. It will help realign your wondering mind. As you do this over and over it will become more natural, and your mind will be clear, and you will get a breakthrough. You will definitely sense the presence of His beauty washing over you. You will become radiant as your gaze is upon the beauty of God.

They looked to Him and were radiant, And their faces were not ashamed.

Psalm 34:5

CHAPTER 8
The Bridal Seal of Fire

She did it! The bride has come to the final chapter (season) in her spiritual journey in the Song of Solomon. Even though she had so many battles and struggles that she faced, she is now going to be seen victorious as she arises from the wilderness. She is portrayed as leaning upon her Beloved!

> *Who is this coming up from the wilderness, Leaning upon her beloved?*
>
> Song of Solomon 8:5

Dependency: The Depth of Bridal Love

Dependency is one of the main reasons why we spend time in the wilderness. Many times we think that God is picking on us and making our lives difficult as we grope in the wilderness. We think He must be disappointed and frustrated with our constant failures, so He puts us in difficult circumstances. We think His patience has run out on us and now He's really going to give us what we deserve. Thankfully, this is not the case for Jesus, the Bridegroom God. He is so far from those lies and accusations. He is actually working everything out for His ultimate pleasure and our ultimate good. It is in the wilderness that God is producing dependency upon Him. He is weakening our own strength and human zeal. He's preparing us for the bridal seal of fire through voluntary weakness.

> *And He said to me, My grace is sufficient for you, for My strength is made perfect in weakness. Therefore most gladly I will rather boast in my infirmities, that the power of Christ may rest upon me. Therefore I take pleasure in infirmities, in reproaches, in needs, in persecutions, in distresses, for Christ's sake. For when I am weak, then I am strong.*
>
> 2 Corinthians 12:9-10

Understanding the Bridal Seal of Fire

All throughout the Song of Solomon, the Bridegroom has been affirming the heart of the Shulamite who has become a mature bride. He has been calling her forth into her prophetic destiny. There are only two times when He makes a request of her. The first request is found in Song of Solomon 2. Jesus asked her to arise and ascend unto the mountains with Him. He wanted her to walk and dance upon all of her present challenges with Him. He was teaching her to trust His effortless leadership over her life. At first, she refused because of fear, but she does say yes in Song of Solomon 4. That simple Yes to do His will even though she felt trapped in her circumstances ravished the heart of the Bridegroom. It was at that moment that changed everything for her. She is being transformed into a mature bride and will no longer be a Shulamite.

Beloved, God moves mountains and does the impossible. He has done it before and you will see Him do it again. He is calling and beckoning you to ascend unto the mountains with Him. He wants to show off His glory as you are at one of the lowest places you have ever been. When you come to a place where you hit rock bottom, you bump into Jesus. When everything around you seems dead and heaven is completely silent, when everything in the natural realm contradicts what you believed, and when it seems there is absolutely no way for your circumstances to change, you are now right at the verge for God to move.

The second request that Jesus makes to the bride is found in Song of Solomon 8. He is going to let her know what He wants from her. I call this the supreme request.

> *Set me as a seal upon your heart, As a seal upon your arm; For love is as strong as death, Jealousy as cruel as the grave; Its flames are flames of fire, most vehement flame. Many waters cannot quench love, Nor can the floods drown it. If a man would give for love All the wealth of his house, It would be utterly despised.*
>
> Song of Solomon 8:6-7

I am sure the Bridegroom wanted to ask this request earlier in the bride's journey, but He knew she was not ready. But now is the set time. She didn't quit or give in while struggling in the wilderness. She kept firm in her identity as a lover of God. So what is Jesus' request to His bride? He asks her to set Him as a seal upon her heart. That's desire at the highest level. The bride does say yes to Jesus request. Her training in the wilderness prepared her for the divine seal of fire. It dawns upon her that everything she had gone through now makes sense.

The bride had passed the greatest test of her life. She now says yes to whatever her Beloved requests from her. **She fully belongs to Him and pledges her allegiance to His leadership**. In chapters 1-4, it was mostly about what she gets from the relationship. That's immaturity. In chapters 5-8, it's about what Jesus gets from the relationship. That's maturity. She is in the relationship for His benefit and ultimate pleasure. She is no longer a Shulamite, but a radiant bride whose heart is conquered by the flame of divine love. It's now about Jesus inheritance in her!

Understanding the Power of the Seal

The Hebrew word for "seal" in Song of Solomon 8:6 is *chowtham*. It means a signet ring. A seal was the emblem of authority worn on the right hand. In the ancient world, kings would put a seal of wax on important documents. They secured them with wax and then stamped the wax with the king's signet ring. The royal seal spoke of the king's ownership, protection, authority, and guarantee that what was on the documents was backed up by all the power of the kingdom. If the royal seal was broken, it was a serious crime that led to the death penalty.

For us personally, the seal is not a seal of an earthly king, but it's the seal of the heavenly King. The seal is about a living Person who's so passionate about taking full ownership over His bride. To set Jesus as the seal upon our heart means we are inviting His fiery love and desire to touch the depths of our inner man, bringing a radical transformation in our lives. It will have a weight of glory and of difficulty upon it. The anointing of heaven will rest upon us, but we will face different types of storms. When our heart is sealed with the Bridegroom's fire, every obstacle will melt before our eyes. Setting Jesus as a seal upon our heart is a statement of giving God that which no one else can give Him – our love. It's the divine exchange between two lovers.

The bridal seal reveals Jesus' passionate love which is stronger than death. That is the strength of the seal. It burns like a mighty flame. You can actually feel the tangible glow of this blaze of fire in your spirit. This kind of love cannot be extinguished or drowned. It's the very flame of Jehovah. He longs to impart His fire into the very core of our being and set us ablaze because He is an all-consuming fire.

> *For the Lord your God is a consuming fire, a jealous God.*
>
> Deuteronomy 4:24

When we come into contact with this bridal seal of fire, we do not remain the same anymore. It enables us to become wholehearted in our pursuit of holy love. There is absolutely no other human being that can offer and impart this seal of fire like Jesus, the Bridegroom God. He held nothing back in His pursuit for the hearts of men. I believe the bridal seal is mostly expressed in Isaiah 53. It reveals the death of the innocent One for the deliverance of the guilty one. It is the greatest chapter on true greatness. The cross is God's relentless passion and desire for humans.

> *Yet it pleased the LORD to bruise (crush) Him; He has put Him to grief. When You make His soul an offering for sin, He shall see His seed, He shall prolong His days, And the pleasure of the LORD shall prosper in His hand. He shall see the labor of His soul, and be satisfied. By His knowledge My righteous Servant shall justify many, For He shall bear their iniquities.*
>
> Isaiah 53:10-11

Jesus was led like a Lamb to the slaughter, and it greatly pleased the Father to bruise and crush His Son at Calvary. Jesus voluntary poured out His soul unto death and gave everything for the sake of love. That's the distinct mark of this bridal seal in Song of Solomon 8. It is why He has the right to ask the request; *Set me as a seal upon your heart, as a seal upon your arm; for love is as strong as death.*

Jesus' love is pictured as being as strong as death. The word strong means powerful, irresistible, mighty and fierce. Death is the strongest and final enemy to be destroyed. It claims everything in the natural realm and is never satisfied. It is very cruel and never feels sorry for anyone. But Jesus' love and passion are as strong as death. It is unyielding like the grave. This is how powerful and strong the love of the Bridegroom God is for His bride. It is why we need to say yes to inviting Jesus' seal of fire to touch our spirit deeply. Amen!

The Power of the Bridal Seal

There is nothing that will overpower Jesus' fiery love. Not even "many waters" can put out the fire of His love. Many waters is a powerful imagery for threatening forces, opposition or difficult circumstances. The enemy will send the waters of disappointment, temptation, hopelessness, loneliness, depression, and grief to try and put out the fire of God in your life. He will tell you that life is not fair and God is not fair. He will tell you that your present struggle will never end, and you're the only one going through this difficult time. But you must not allow the enemy to try and drown you with the waters and floods of life. I believe you will stay steady because you're a fighter and are stronger than you think. You will keep your gaze upon the One who's fighting for you. He will never let you down. Trust Him knowing that everything is going to be ok.

In the midst of persecution, temptation, and even martyrdom, the heart that is sealed with fiery love will not be moved, shaken or separated. It will be a heart that conquers through Christ. It was Paul the Apostle who received this revelation in his life.

> *Who shall separate us from the love of Christ? Shall tribulation, or distress, or persecution, or famine, or nakedness, or peril, or sword? As it is written: "For Your sake we are killed all day long; We are accounted as sheep for the slaughter." Yet in all these things we are more than conquerors through Him who loved us. For I am persuaded that neither death nor life, nor angels nor principalities nor powers, nor things*

> *present nor things to come, nor height nor depth, nor any other created thing, shall be able to separate us from the love of God which is in Christ Jesus our Lord.*
>
> Romans 8:35-39

As the bride receives the seal upon her heart, she is now fully obeying Jesus without any regard to cost. There were probably some times in her journey when she obeyed because she had to. She probably thought she was paying the price to love Jesus with all of her heart. But now she is a voluntary lover who has no price tags. She doesn't recognize sacrifice. It is a profound joy and delight. There are no pockets of resistance within her. She is fully her Beloveds and is in the relationship for Him and His glory. It's about what He wants and desires, and not what she wants and desires. The power to love Jesus is her reward. At the beginning of her journey in Song of Solomon 1, she asked for the kiss of Jesus to awaken her dull heart, but now she's fully empowered to love Him in Song of Solomon 8. What an amazing transformation that has taken place in her life and journey!

Believers without the revelation of Jesus' blazing love for them are the ones who will count the cost. They seem to serve out of duty rather than delight. Whatever sacrifice or struggle you are going through cannot compare to the beauty and power of the Bridegroom's seal of fire. He is worth more than any sacrifice. Worthy is the Lamb! If you think paying the price is a struggle for you, then take some time and meditate upon this portion of scripture. It will realign your thought process.

> *But what things were gain to me, these I have counted loss for Christ. Yet indeed I also count all things loss for the excellence of the knowledge of Christ Jesus my Lord, for whom I have suffered the loss of all things, and count them*

> *as rubbish, that I may gain Christ and be found in Him, not having my own righteousness, which is from the law, but that which is through faith in Christ, the righteousness which is from God by faith; that I may know Him and the power of His resurrection, and the fellowship of His sufferings, being conformed to His death.*
>
> Philippians 3:7-10

Four Aspects of the Bridal Seal

1. It imparts the glory of Jesus' passionate love which is strong as death in our hearts. It is what empowers and tenderizes us to love God more. Jesus Himself is the living seal of divine fire. When we say yes to His loving request, our heart will become fully His. The relationship will be about what benefits Him, and what makes Him happy.

2. It burns away the dross and purges all that gets in the way of the pursuit of holy love. This can become painful at times but is necessary so we can become a prepared bride on the last day.

3. It delivers God's people who are in bondage just like it did for the children of Israel in Exodus 2. It was Moses who encountered the burning bush that would not go out. God raised him up to become a deliverer of His passionate fire.

4. It will utterly destroy the enemies of the worthy Lamb of God. His fire will consume them.

The bridal seal of fire is powerful. It is a mighty weapon coming from the very throne of God. It is the completion of our journey to wholehearted love. To have this supernatural fire abiding in our heart doesn't come overnight. Just as it took the Shulamite eight chapters (seasons) to receive this seal of fire and become the bride, so it will take time for us to get it as well. There will be a struggle and wrestle during our pursuit, but there is no true victory without a fight. The Father will not relent until He has a bride burning with the seal of His Son's own relentless fire. He wants us to love Him as He loves us in our relationship with Him. He has promised to give His Son an eternal companion as His inheritance – a bride who voluntarily chooses to be equally yoked with Him in love. This will be the glory of Jesus' wedding day. It is the great prize of all ages that He awaits.

The Bridal Seal: The Marriage of the Lamb

The bridal seal of fire finds it's consummation at the marriage of the Lamb. Redemption finds its fulfillment in a Hallelujah chorus, a wedding feast, and a bride dressed in pure white. In Revelation 19, we see the literal end of our journey in this age and the beginning of the next. It is the greatest picture of what true love is all about. You cannot have any higher price than God giving Himself for love.

Beloved, you have been invited to the most glorious wedding by the most powerful and influential person on the planet. The slain Lamb is going to stun and surprise you. It will be the greatest "Wow" you will have ever uttered. His eyes are upon you right now. His heart is captured by your loving devotion towards Him. **Get ready; the Bridegroom is coming to the earth**. We will be resurrected one glorious day. We will be caught up to meet the Lord in the sky and will be instantly changed. The groaning of creation will be satisfied when our body is transformed into the likeness of His radiant body. We as the bride will have a body just like His.

> *He has the power to bring everything under his control. By His power He will change our earthly bodies. They will become like His glorious body.*
>
> Philippians 3:21 (NIRV)

Just as Jesus ascended, so you will ascend. Just as He reigns, so you will reign. Your greatness abides in the resurrection of the Son of God. Do you believe that you will bear the image of the Man from heaven? That means you will be just like Him.

> *And just as we have borne the image of the earthly man, so shall we bear the image of the heavenly Man.*
>
> 1 Corinthians 15:49 (NIV)

This is our destiny. It is where our spiritual journey through many seasons has led us. It's why Jesus is so passionate and determined to seal us with the bridal seal of fire. We will be dressed in clean and bright garments before the throne. Gladness and rejoicing will be our portion forever and ever. We say YES to the bridal seal of fire. We say YES to be fully prepared for the marriage of the Lamb. Hallelujah!

> *And I heard, as it were, the voice of a great multitude, as the sound of many waters and as the sound of mighty thundering's, saying, "Hallelujah! For the Lord God Omnipotent reigns! Let us be glad and rejoice and give Him glory, for the marriage of the Lamb has come, and His wife has made herself ready." And to her it was granted to be arrayed in fine linen, clean and bright, for the fine linen is the righteous acts of the saints.*
>
> Revelation 19:6-8

CHAPTER 9
The Worthy Lamb of God

Revelation 5 is a very distinct and important chapter to understand. It unveils one of the most moving passages describing the suffering and reign of the Lamb of God, who is coming to judge and rule the earth in power and glory. It's the highest expression of heavenly worship that says with a loud voice: "Worthy is the Lamb."

> *And I saw in the right hand of Him who sat on the throne a scroll written inside and on the back, sealed with seven seals. Then I saw a strong angel proclaiming with a loud voice, "Who is worthy to open the scroll and to loose its seals?" And no one in heaven or on the earth or under the earth was able to open the scroll, or to look at it. So I wept much, because no one was found worthy to open and read the scroll, or to look at it. But one of the elders said to me, "Do not weep. Behold, the Lion of the tribe of Judah, the Root of David, has prevailed to open the scroll and to loose its seven seals." And I looked, and behold, in the midst of the throne and of the four living creatures, and in the midst of the elders, stood a Lamb as though it had been slain, having seven horns and seven eyes, which are the seven Spirits of God sent out into all the earth. Then He came and took the scroll out of the right hand of Him who sat on the throne. Now when*

He had taken the scroll, the four living creatures and the twenty-four elders fell down before the Lamb, each having a harp, and golden bowls full of incense, which are the prayers of the saints. And they sang a new song, saying: "You are worthy to take the scroll, And to open its seals; For You were slain, And have redeemed us to God by Your blood Out of every tribe and tongue and people and nation, And have made us kings and priests to our God; And we shall reign on the earth." Then I looked, and I heard the voice of many angels around the throne, the living creatures, and the elders; and the number of them was ten thousand times ten thousand, and thousands of thousands, saying with a loud voice: "Worthy is the Lamb who was slain To receive power and riches and wisdom, And strength and honor and glory and blessing!" And every creature which is in heaven and on the earth and under the earth and such as are in the sea, and all that are in them, I heard saying: "Blessing and honor and glory and power Be to Him who sits on the throne, And to the Lamb, forever and ever!" Then the four living creatures said, "Amen!" And the twenty-four elders fell down and worshiped Him who lives forever and ever.

Revelation 5:1-14

The Definition of the Scroll

John the Apostle sees and hears the roar of a strong angel proclaiming, "who is worthy to open the scroll and to loose its seals?" I believe this prophetic question was like a magnet that was drawing and pulling John in, as he pondered over one of the greatest questions of the ages. I'm sure his mind was racing everywhere to think of an answer. And I'm sure the last thing he wanted to hear was that "no one" was able to open the scroll or to look at it.

So what was John's response to the two devastating words "no one" was able to open the scroll? He starts weeping intensely for some time. For the ninety-year-old Apostle to be weeping over the fact that no one was found worthy to open the scroll shows the utter significance and importance of it. He wept because the consummation of history would now be indefinitely postponed.

The scroll is the title deed of the earth and the action plan of God to reap the great harvest. It reveals how God will manifest His righteous vindication to those who reject His Son. It expresses the deepest emotions of God's heart. As the scroll is unrolled, it's going to create such calamity on the earth. When the scroll is opened the drama unfolds!

The Lamb is Worthy

As John continued weeping, he hears one of the twenty-four elders tell him to stop weeping but to "behold" the Lion of the tribe of Judah who has prevailed to open and lose the seven seals. As he peers across the throne room of heaven, to his surprise, he sees a Lamb standing with scars and wounds upon His body. **He went from weeping to stunned**. He must have been so encouraged when he was given this message from heaven, that the Lion had prevailed and the Lamb was found worthy to open the scroll. It's the great dance and drama of the Lion and the Lamb!

The word "worthy" means to be qualified, deserving, capable, and to have earned the right. It's an elite position in God's order. Only the Lamb before the throne of God was found worthy to take the scroll from the Father and open it. He alone has the intelligence, understanding, wisdom, and power as a human to administer the end time judgments. He is qualified and has been commissioned by the Father to judge the earth. He is coming with eyes of liquid fire on a gorgeous white stallion to make war, conquering sin and evil across the earth. He is the Bridegroom judge!

> *Now I saw heaven opened, and behold, a white horse. And He who sat on him was called Faithful and True, and in righteousness He judges and makes war. His eyes were like a flame of fire, and on His head were many crowns. He had a name written that no one knew except Himself. He was clothed with a robe dipped in blood, and His name is called The Word of God. And the armies in heaven, clothed in fine linen, white and clean, followed Him on white horses. Now out of His mouth goes a sharp sword, that with it He should strike the nations. And He Himself will rule them with a rod of iron. He Himself treads the winepress of the fierceness and wrath of Almighty God. And He has on His robe and on His thigh a name written: KING OF KINGS AND LORD OF LORDS.*
>
> Revelation 19:11-16

The more we understand the Lamb being found worthy before the Father and all the angels of heaven, the greater we will adore the heart of God. Adoration for the Lamb is what moves heaven. It ravishes His heart. The cry worthy is the power of adoration! Through all our pain and suffering the Lamb of God will be worth it all.

The Lamb is pictured as being slain in the midst of the throne. **He still bears the marks of slaughter in heaven**. It is why we see the angels, living creatures, and the twenty-four elders crying with a loud voice; *Worthy is the lamb who was slain.* The Lamb was despised by man, yet billions of angels worship and adore Him. He was rejected, yet He sits at the right hand of God the Father. Kings upon the earth will be speechless before Him.

In Revelation 7, we see a great multitude which no one could number from all nations standing before the throne and the Lamb. This is prophetic worship at its best. I so love the Lamb of God.

> *After these things I looked, and behold, a great multitude which no one could number, of all nations, tribes, peoples, and tongues, standing before the throne and before the Lamb, clothed with white robes, with palm branches in their hands, and crying out with a loud voice, saying, "Salvation belongs to our God who sits on the throne, and to the Lamb!" All the angels stood around the throne and the elders and the four living creatures, and fell on their faces before the throne and worshiped God, saying: Amen! Blessing and glory and wisdom, Thanksgiving and honor and power and might, Be to our God forever and ever. Amen.*
>
> Revelation 7:9-12

So why was Jesus the Lamb slain? What motivated the uncreated God to step out of eternity and go through the hassle and suffering by becoming a human, and die on the cross? It's because He wanted to betroth Himself to us forever (see Hosea 2:19). He wanted to have a voluntary bride partnering with Him in close fellowship. He wanted a lover, someone who would absolutely adore Him with no strings attached. He wanted someone who would climb mountains with Him just to be with Him. He wanted someone who would gladly surrender to His will, trusting His leadership, even in the midst of the storm. He wanted someone who smiles at the thought of Him. That's the message being communicated that the Lamb was slain, found worthy before the throne, and is coming back to rule the earth in raging power and glory.

I believe it's important to understand the most powerful and influential song that is sung before the throne: "Worthy is the Lamb!" This glorious song in heaven sounds like a huge angelic choir, singing in perfect harmony. There are actually three worthy songs in the book of Revelation. You can study and meditate upon them in a much deeper way.

3 Worthy Songs in Revelation 4 & 5

The first worthy song is sung to the Father in heaven. This chapter is devoted to God the Father upon His throne.

> *"<u>You are worthy, O Lord</u>, To receive glory and honor and power; For You created all things, And by Your will they exist and were created."*
>
> Revelation 4:11

The second worthy song is sung to the Son of God. He alone was found worthy to take the scroll from the Father and loose its seals.

> *Now when He had taken the scroll, the four living creatures and the twenty-four elders fell down before the Lamb, each having a harp, and golden bowls full of incense, which are the prayers of the saints. And they sang a new song, saying: "<u>You are worthy to take the scroll</u>, And to open its seals; For You were slain, And have redeemed us to God by Your blood Out of every tribe and tongue and people and nation,*
>
> Revelation 5:8-9

The third worthy song is also sung to the Son of God. What a stunning sight to behold. Because the Lamb is worthy before the throne, He alone receives the sevenfold anointing of power, riches, wisdom, strength, honor, glory, and blessing.

> *Then I looked, and I heard the voice of many angels around the throne, the living creatures, and the elders; and the number of them was ten thousand times ten thousand, and thousands of thousands, saying with a loud voice: "<u>Worthy is the</u>*

> *<u>Lamb who was slain</u> To receive power and riches and wisdom, And strength and honor and glory and blessing!"*
>
> Revelation 5:11-12

The Beauty of the Lamb of God

There is no one who compares or comes close to the beauty of the Lamb's heart and leadership. The Lamb represents meekness, defenselessness, and vulnerability. The Greek word for Lamb is *arnion* which is translated "Lambkin." It means poor little thing. The Greek word for antichrist is *therion* which is translated as "beast." It means great vicious monster. So we have the heavyweight championship – arnion vs. therion.

The Lamb's defenselessness is His Lion-like strength. His suffering on the cross is His victory. He bears the marks of slaughter upon Him. He paid the highest price, so you could know Him. His fragrance fills the entire city of the New Jerusalem and causes angelic beings to prostrate before Him. He appears at the center of the drama in the book of Revelation. **The Lamb is God's heavyweight champion**. He is unchallenged and undefeated. The scriptures call Him the Bright and Morning Star.

> *"I, Jesus, have sent My angel to testify to you these things in the churches. I am the Root and the Offspring of David, the Bright and Morning Star." And the Spirit and the bride say, "Come!" And let him who hears say, "Come!" And let him who thirsts come. Whoever desires, let him take the water of life freely.*
>
> Revelation 22:16-17

The Lamb's appearance was marred more than any other man. The Living Bible says He was beaten so bad you could not even recognize Him as a person (see Isaiah 52:14). But the good news is He is alive on the throne of God. My champion's not dead. He is the greatest leader on the face of the earth. His influence has far surpassed any great kings and rulers of the earth. They will bow in utter silence before Him. They will see how powerless they are and how powerful He is when they behold Him.

Jesus had no desire to be recognized before man as He lived under the audience of One. He entered His ministry on a wild donkey into Jerusalem but will come back on a white horse to take full dominion over the nations. He had no desire to appear equal to God in the eyes of men and veiled His glory as He came to the earth. As a human, He considered our souls of greater worth and value than the costly humility of taking on humanity. He didn't just sign up for thirty-three years, but for all eternity. He gave up the shining brilliance of heaven's glory. He made Himself of no reputation. He came to unveil His Father's glory while veiling His own glory. He was considered the illegitimate son of a carpenter and was called a drunkard. He could have come to Rome instead of Bethlehem. He could have been born of a wealthy and noble family, but this wasn't His strategy. **When He had all the glory, He gladly laid it aside.** He is the radiance of perfect love. From the manger to the cross He walked a path of humiliation. From the manger to the cross He burned with the radiance of a servant's heart. How can the Creator humble Himself before those He created? Jesus went from the very highest place to the very lowest place. He went from the place of perfect sinlessness to the place of perfect darkness. He went from being enthroned above the cherubim to a barn smelling with urine and dung. We have no concept of the gap between heaven and earth. We have no idea of what it was like for Jesus to take this rigorous path. He went all the way into a life of radical obedience. The cross was the goal of His incarnation, and the New Jerusalem coming to the earth is the reward for His Father. He's called the Lamb who was led to the slaughter. No one has ever died this way. His birth was unique, His life as a human on the earth was unique, and His death was unique. It's why the seraphim cry, "Worthy is the Lamb."

Beloved, there is none like Jesus, the Lamb of God. Because He was found worthy before the Father, He will take dominion over the earth, and we will serve Him with a heart of love and adoration. His kingdom is everlasting. It will never be shaken. And because He's the King of His kingdom, He will do according to His will in heaven.

> *For His dominion is an everlasting dominion, and His kingdom is from generation to generation. All the inhabitants of the earth are reputed as nothing; He does according to His will in the army of heaven And among the inhabitants of the earth.*
>
> Daniel 4:35

Different Faces of the Lamb of God

Let's look at some different faces of who the Lamb of God is in the Book of Revelation. I encourage you to study, meditate and anchor yourself in these divine truths. You will not be disappointed in the worthy Lamb of God. He is the name that angels love and adore!

1. The Lamb is a Lion.
But one of the elders said to me, "Do not weep. Behold, the Lion of the tribe of Judah, the Root of David, has prevailed to open the scroll and to loose its seven seals."

Revelation 5:5

2. He is a Lamb.
And I looked, and behold, in the midst of the throne and of the four living creatures, and in the midst of the elders, stood a Lamb as though it had been slain, having seven horns and seven eyes, which are the seven Spirits of God sent out into all the earth.

Revelation 5:6

3. The Lamb is a wounded Lover.
And I looked, and behold, in the midst of the throne and of the four living creatures, and in the midst of the elders, stood a Lamb as though it had been slain, having seven horns and seven eyes, which are the seven Spirits of God sent out into all the earth.

Revelation 5:6

4. The Lamb is worthy of all worship.
Saying with a loud voice: "Worthy is the Lamb who was slain To receive power and riches and wisdom, And strength and honor and glory and blessing!" And every creature which is in heaven and on the earth and under the earth and such as are in the sea, and all that are in them, I heard saying: "Blessing and honor and glory and power Be to Him who sits on the throne, And to the Lamb, forever and ever!"

Revelation 5:12-13

After these things I looked, and behold, a great multitude which no one could number, of all nations, tribes, peoples, and tongues, standing before the throne and before the Lamb, clothed with white robes, with palm branches in their hands, and crying out with a loud voice, saying, "Salvation belongs to our God who sits on the throne, and to the Lamb!" All the angels stood around the throne and the elders and the four living creatures, and fell on their faces before the throne and worshiped God, saying: "Amen! Blessing and glory and wisdom, Thanksgiving and honor and power and might, Be to our God forever and ever. Amen..."For the Lamb who is in the midst of the throne will shepherd them and lead them to living fountains of waters .And God will wipe away every tear from their eyes."

Revelation 7:9-12, 17

5. The Lamb is the judge of all the earth.
Now I saw when the Lamb opened one of the seals; and I heard one of the four living creatures saying with a voice like thunder, "Come and see." And I looked, and behold, a white horse. He who sat on it had a

bow; and a crown was given to him, and he went out conquering and to conquer.

Revelation 6:1-2

6. The Lamb is our total cleansing and forgiveness.
And I said to him, "Sir, you know." So he said to me, These are the ones who come out of the great tribulation, and washed their robes and made them white in the blood of the Lamb.

Revelation 7:14

7. The Lamb is our Shepherd.
For the Lamb who is in the midst of the throne will shepherd them and lead them to living fountains of waters. And God will wipe away every tear from their eyes.

Revelation 7:17

8. The Lamb is the Overcomer.
And they overcame him by the blood of the Lamb and by the word of their testimony, and they did not love their lives to the death.

Revelation 12:11

9. The Lamb is the greatest leader in human history.
Then I looked, and behold, a Lamb standing on Mount Zion, and with Him one hundred and forty-four thousand, having His Father's name written on their foreheads. And I heard a voice from heaven, like the voice of many waters, and like the voice of loud thunder. And I heard the sound of harpists playing their harps. They sang as it were a new song before the throne, before the four living creatures, and the elders; and no one could learn that song except the hundred and forty-four thousand who were redeemed from the earth. These are the ones who were not defiled with women, for they are virgins. <u>These are the ones who follow the Lamb wherever He goes</u>. These were redeemed from among men, being firstfruits to God and to the Lamb. And in their mouth was found no deceit, for they are without fault before the throne of God.

Revelation 14:1-5

10. The Lamb's presence is powerful.

He himself (anyone who worships the beast and his image, and receives his mark on his forehead or on his head) *shall also drink of the wine of the wrath of God, which is poured out full strength into the cup of His indignation. He shall be tormented with fire and brimstone in the presence of the holy angels and in the presence of the Lamb.*

Revelation 14:10

11. The Lamb is the Song of all ages.

Then I saw another sign in heaven, great and marvelous: seven angels having the seven last plagues, for in them the wrath of God is complete. And I saw something like a sea of glass mingled with fire, and those who have the victory over the beast, over his image and over his mark and over the number of his name, standing on the sea of glass, having harps of God. They sing the song of Moses, the servant of God, and the song of the Lamb, saying: "Great and marvelous are Your works, Lord God Almighty! Just and true are Your ways, O King of the saints! Who shall not fear You, O Lord, and glorify Your name? For You alone are holy. For all nations shall come and worship before You, For Your judgments have been manifested."

Revelation 15:1-4

12. The Lamb is the Lord of Lords and King of Kings.

These will make war with the Lamb, and the Lamb will overcome them, for He is Lord of lords and King of kings; and those who are with Him are called, chosen, and faithful.

Revelation 17:14

13. The Lamb has a stunning wedding prepared for His bride.

Then he said to me, "Write: 'Blessed are those who are called to the marriage supper of the Lamb!'" And he said to me, "These are the true sayings of God."

Revelation 19:9

14. The Lamb is the foundation of the eternal city.
Now the wall of the city had twelve foundations, and on them were the names of the twelve apostles of the Lamb.

Revelation 21:14

15. The Lamb is the temple in the Heavenly Jerusalem.
But I saw no temple in it, for the Lord God Almighty and the Lamb are its temple.

Revelation 21:22

16. The Lamb is the Light in the New Jerusalem.
The city had no need of the sun or the moon to shine in it, for the glory of God illuminated it. The Lamb is its light.

Revelation 21:23

17. The Lamb is the only way to salvation.
But there shall by no means enter it anything that defiles, or causes an abomination or a lie, but only those who are written in the Lamb's Book of Life.

Revelation 21:27

18. The Lamb is the pure river of water of life.
And he showed me a pure river of water of life, clear as crystal, proceeding from the throne of God and of the Lamb.

Revelation 22:1

19. The Lamb will have His servant's gladly serve Him.
And there shall be no more curse, but the throne of God and of the Lamb shall be in it, and His servants shall serve Him.

Revelation 22:3

20. The Lamb is coming to the earth to reward His bride.
"And behold, I am coming quickly, and My reward is with Me, to give to everyone according to his work. I am the Alpha and the Omega, the Beginning and the End, the First and the Last."

Revelation 22:12-13

Destined to Crown the Worthy Lamb of God

The bride of Christ is destined to crown the slain Lamb. He is worthy and deserving to be crowned with our love. It was the Lamb who first crowned us. To wear a crown near God's throne is the greatest honor that can be given. We don't just cast these crowns anywhere, but we cast them before the feet of the Lamb of God. This is where I want to spend my life expressing my love for Him. **He deserves the reward of His suffering**!

One of the best ways we can crown the worthy Lamb is to live completely for Him alone, and His pleasure. It's called passion for Jesus, and loving Him with all of our heart. It's time to let go of our personal agendas and begin to pursue His agenda. The Lamb's agenda does have pain and suffering along the journey. We tread the same path that He tread. We follow the Lamb wherever He goes. But His agenda also has a realm of glory and fire. It's exhilarating. Jesus the Lamb will be worth the persecution, suffering, and agony. There is a realm of glory that we will possess. Nothing in life even compares to it. It's priceless!

> *For I consider that the sufferings of this present time are not worthy to be compared with the glory which shall be revealed in us.*
>
> Romans 8:18

I don't think we fully understand the hidden mystery of suffering and tribulation. Only the Lamb fully knows what He is doing and sees the big picture of our life. He takes our relationship with Him seriously. It's not a game but is genuine and real. He is not just looking out for our comfort, but He's looking out to who He's transforming us into. During the process, it will be painful at times, but He wants us to fully submit to His amazing leadership. Do you believe He wants us to be entrusted with authority to reign not only in this life but during the millennial reign? This is where He's taking His bride!

> *To the one who is victorious and does my will to the end, I will give authority over the nations*— *that one 'will rule them with an iron scepter and will dash them to pieces like pottery'—just as I have received authority from my Father. I will also give that one the morning star.*
>
> Revelation 2:26-28 (NIV)

Tribulation is the pathway to crowns. It is the door to triumph. Crowns are cast in crucibles, and the gold of godly character is found at the feet of the Lamb. It's forged in the flame of earthly trials. No one wins the greatest victory until he has walked the winepress of woes. The steps that lead to thrones are stained with spattered blood, and scars are the price for scepters. We will wrestle our crowns from the giants we conquer. It is no secret that grief has always been the companion of the great. I like what Frank Laubach says about greatness: "The Lord will not wish to count my trophies but my scars." The Lamb is making us a vessel of new wine, a fragrant offering. Hallelujah!

The End of our Journey – the Marriage of the Lamb

As we already peered into the marriage of the Lamb in Revelation 19, I want to spend a little more time developing this grand theme. It's what passion for Jesus is all about!

Just as weddings have taken place all throughout church history, so there will be an ultimate wedding – the marriage of the Lamb. It will be the culmination of the ages.

> *And I heard, as it were, the voice of a great multitude, as the sound of many waters and as the sound of mighty thunderings, saying, "Halleluia! For the Lord God Omnipotent reigns! Let us be glad and rejoice and give Him glory, for the marriage of the Lamb has come, and His wife has made herself ready." And to her it was granted to be arrayed in fine linen, clean and bright, for the fine linen is the righteous acts of the saints. Then he said to me, "Write: 'Blessed are those who are called to the marriage supper of the Lamb!'" And he said to me, "These are the true sayings of God."*
>
> Revelation 19:6-9

Besides the cross and the resurrection, I believe that Jesus' wedding day will be the greatest and happiest day for Him. He has waited so patiently for this glorious day. He looks forward to it with such excitement and anticipation. The Lamb will be the One wearing the wedding crown. We will see Him being crowned as the beautiful King!

> <u>*Your eyes will see the King in His beauty;*</u> *They will see the land that is very far off.*
>
> Isaiah 33:17

Jesus, the worthy Lamb, is coming soon to make you His eternal companion. He will have an equally yoked bride that is sealed and marked for His wedding day. You will be His forever because He pursued you. Somebody believed in you and did something about it. **Somebody fought for your freedom.** Someone is coming to get you. Someone is preparing a gorgeous, gigantic city for you.

> *But now they desire a better, that is, a heavenly country. Therefore God is not ashamed to be called their God, for He has prepared a city for them.*
>
> Hebrews 11:16

Jesus the wounded Lamb, paid a great price so we can be invited to the marriage of the lamb. His path was marked with wounds, and the future destiny of the bride is marked with glory. The bride on the last day is soaring and rejoicing with a glad heart because she sees the wisdom of how God led her through the wilderness. She will have a clear understanding of how all of her circumstances were divinely arranged by the King Himself. It is part of the preparation for the wedding day. When the end time bride of Christ stands upon the crystal sea of glass, everything will all make sense before the Lamb and His throne.

It is very important that we are found prepared for this glorious day. We don't want to have any "regrets" when we behold the Lamb in His glorious palace. We want to stand with confidence and a heart full of love and adoration. Are you preparing for the great wedding of the worthy Lamb? What are some practical things you are doing to have your heart equipped and made ready to meet Jesus face to face? Think about it and take some time to wait upon the Lord, and let Him shine His light upon you to let you know. He will be faithful. He is more committed to you than you are to Him. He wants you shining in pure radiance when you see His face!

> *They shall see His face, and His name shall be on their foreheads. There shall be no night there: They need no lamp nor light of the sun, for the Lord God gives them light. And they shall reign forever and ever.*
>
> Revelation 22:4-5

Beloved, heaven is coming to the earth. Jesus will have a bride made ready for His wedding day. He will share His authority with us in divine partnership. He will let us sit with Him on His holy throne. Think about that! The Lamb is not threatened to share His government with His bride.

> *Behold, I stand at the door and knock. If anyone hears My voice and opens the door, I will come to him and dine with him, and he with Me. To him who overcomes I will grant to sit with Me on My throne, as I also overcame and sat down with My Father on His throne.*
>
> Revelation 3:20-21

There is going to be a wedding! You will be made ready and prepared as a radiant bride. You will love and worship the Lamb all throughout your spiritual pilgrimage on this side of eternity. You will carry and impart the passionate flame of God's love and beauty to a hurting world. Passion for Jesus will be your testimony. **Passion for Jesus will be the banner over your lives**. Remember, passion for Jesus comes from discovering His passion for you!

> *And we have known and believed the love that God has for us. God is love, and he who abides in love abides in God, and God in him. Love has been perfected among us in this: that we may have boldness in the day of judgment; because as He is, so are we in this world. There is no fear in love; but perfect love casts out fear, because fear involves torment. But he who fears has not been made perfect in love. <u>We love Him because He first loved us</u>.*
>
> 1 John 4:16-19

OTHER PRODUCTS BY MIKE BRUMBACK

BOOKS

THE SHULAMITE'S CRY portrays the journey of the Shulamite who is being trained in the wilderness to become Jesus' bride. In chapters 1-4, it's mostly about what benefits her in the relationship with Jesus the Bridegroom. In chapters 5-8, it's mostly about what benefits Jesus the Beloved. She is now in the relationship for His pleasure. She will be seen coming up out of the wilderness, leaning upon her Beloved, and sealed with the fire of Jesus' surpassing love.

THE SHULAMITE'S CRY
Available in Korean

ENCOUNTERING THE THRONE OF GOD
This is a verse by verse study guide of Revelation 4. It unveils the glory and majesty of the throne room of heaven. It peers into the three distinct diamonds (jasper, sardius, emerald) which reflects who God the Father is. You will be absolutely fascinated and will marvel at the greatness and majesty of the throne of God.

More...

THE BEAUTY OF THE CROSS – Take another look at the heart of the Father over His Son from eternity past. It's a journey of passion, determination and mercy for broken and sinful mankind. Jesus is a real person with real feelings and struggles, and fully identifies with us. He faced overwhelming pain, rejection, betrayal, abandonment, loneliness, and was constantly misunderstood. As we peer into the bloody crucifixion and supernatural resurrection, we discover the story of a triumphant, conquering king who is preparing His bride for a grand wedding, and will reign with Him.

CDS

THRONE OF GOD is an anointed CD that focuses on the beauty and majesty of God the Father in the throne room of heaven. It is combined with music, prophetic singers and inspirational prayers in the 'harp & bowl' model. Both singers Julie Myer and Paula Bowers, flow so well as they sing about the jasper God in Revelation 4.

THRONE OF GOD 2 is a wonderful CD that has 'harp & bowl' worship with different worship leaders and singers from the International House of Prayer of Kansas City.

ONLY YOU is a 'harp & bowl' worship CD in both English and Korean. It was produced in Kansas City but most of the worship leaders and singers are from Korea. It is a great CD that will awaken your heart to love God more.

CONTACT INFO
FOR MIKE BRUMBACK

MAIL
Mike Brumback
401 S. Gallaher View Road #177
Knoxville, TN 37919

PHONE
865-456-5970

EMAIL
brumbackmb@passionforjesusnow.com

WEBSITE
www.passionforjesusnow.com

Made in the USA
San Bernardino, CA
23 October 2018